INTERTWINING

Published by
Princeton Architectural Press
37 East 7th Street
New York, New York 10003
212.995.9620

For a free catalog of books,
call 1.800.722.6657

Editing and layout:
Clare Jacobson and Molly Blieden
Special thanks to: Caroline Green, Therese Kelly, Bill Monaghan, Mark Lamster, Allison Saltzman, and Ann C. Urban—Kevin C. Lippert, publisher

Library of Congress
Cataloging-in-Publication Data

Holl, Steven
    Intertwining : selected projects 1989–1995 /
Steven Holl.
        p.   cm.
    Includes bibliographical references.
    ISBN 1-56898-061-2 (cloth : alk. paper)
    1. Holl, Steven—Themes, motives.
2. Architecture, Modern—20th century—United States—Themes, motives. I. Title.
NA737.H56A4 1996
720'.92—dc20   95-45137
                                CIP

INTERTWINING

STEVEN HOLL
SELECTED PROJECTS 1989–1995

PRINCETON ARCHITECTURAL PRESS

To Janet Olmsted Cross

ACKNOWLEDGEMENTS

In a Manhattan landscape of strange indifference, Professor Kenneth Frampton, Lebbeus Woods, Vito Acconci, Andrew MacNair, as well as artist-poets Arakawa and Madeline Gins, have been critical colleagues. In Japan it has helped me to have the support and confidence of Tadao Ando, Arata Isozaki, and Toyo Ito. Toshio Nakamura has been a mysterious saint of a publisher. In Europe the critical friendship of Rem Koolhaas and Juhani Pallasmaa have been essential. These pages would be impossible without Kevin Lippert's continued support and the contributions of Janet Cross, Clare Jacobson, and Molly Blieden.

FOREWORD

Steven Holl

Anchoring, published in 1989, documents the architectural work of our office from 1975 to 1988. The argument for an architecture formed according to each unique site and situation remains central to our work. Through anchoring, architecture condenses meaning into the particular history of the site—its ground, locale, region—with the functional and social program.

During the past seven years (1988–95) our office has been involved with projects in a variety of locations including Japan, Finland, Germany, Switzerland, Holland, Korea, and Norway. These experiences reinforce my convictions about anchoring architecture to the history of site. This philosophy is fundamental to developing concepts for a relevant, meaningful architecture in a time when architects travel around the world more than ever, when many countries commission foreign architects, and when architecture is becoming increasingly cut off from basic principles that form its local and global relevance. The challenge of extremely diverse lands, cultures, climates, and their urban or suburban conditions sets still new obligations for anchored architecture.

We also are concerned with exploring the essential experiences of day-to-day phenomena. Ordinary and extraordinary facts, circumstances, and experiences, when seen as important, can generate a meaningful architecture. If *Anchoring* argued for a universal in the specific, an absolute in the relative, a second, related argument has been building through our other works and publications, such as *Questions of Perception* in 1994 with Alberto Pérez-Gómez and Juhani Pallasmaa. In this second chapter of theoretical and practical work, an "architecture of intertwining" is connected with a phenomenal architecture of everyday experience. One is grounded in and out of situation; the other illuminated by sensory, perceptual, conceptual, and emotional experiences.

INTRODUCTION

Alberto Pérez-Gómez

Maurice Merleau-Ponty's life-long interest in perception, as expressed in the technical language of his *Phenomenology of Perception* and the more poetic notes of his *The Visible and the Invisible*, proposed an important challenge for architects. He stated succinctly that something is definitely wrong in our culture if what one can say *about* perception is more interesting than perception itself. In his work he demonstrated that perception, and humanity's understanding of meaning, is an event far more mysterious than our deterministic scientific models have ever been able to grasp. Seemingly commonsense "assumptions"—such as the hegemony of linear temporality, where there is no "presence," and the homogeneity of geometric space; or the identity of depth with "the other two" dimensions (breadth and height)—are shown to be merely partial truths, misconceptions that often hide the potential richness of our experience.

This suggests, indeed, the possibility of an architecture that may be capable of both revealing and constituting itself through *experience* as a nonidealized notion, without nevertheless denying its copresence with language. The notion of experience could be, and indeed has been, interpreted idealistically. While for Jacques Derrida and his followers the very notion of experience is still part of the metaphysics of presence, for Merleau-Ponty in *The Visible and the Invisible* the goal was precisely to nonidealize the notion of experience. The

"denial" of experience is impossible, a philosophical nonsense. Experience presupposes nothing more than an encounter between "us" and "what is." As if in response to Derrida, Merleau-Ponty argued that a resolution to ask of experience its secret was *already* an idealist commitment. Indeed our relationship with the things of the world is never "free" of meaning; our life, this "intertwining," is a network of reciprocities (I only truly know myself through the "other"); moreover, reality is not reducible to the conventional poles of objectivity and subjectivity, it is a gift to a non-dualistic, embodied consciousness—the whole, experiencing human body as a synesthetic receptor.

The fact that we may now believe that meanings are simply mental associations, that space is "out there" and merely quantitative (describable through three-dimensional coordinates), or that decontextualized images (in cyberspace) *are* reality, has precipitated the world of architectural practice into a crisis that makes Merleau-Ponty's challenge crucial and timely. The challenge must be addressed as a critical practice that endeavors to recover the mystery of the ordinary and makes manifest the eloquent heterogeneity of depth.

This is the challenge that Steven Holl has turned into a self-conscious philosophical program for his most recent work. Engaged as he has been in a prolific practice, this is indeed no small task. Precisely because their considerations are never merely stylistic, diverse build-

ing projects necessarily offer different possibilities for this mode of practice.

Obviously Holl's work reveals a careful consideration of materiality, light, color, and texture. It should be remarked, however, that if the sensuous aspect of architecture is crucial in his work, this is not an end in itself, but a means to engage the inhabitant's imagination. Despite our contemporary skepticism about the eloquence of "presence," artists and poets, both traditional and contemporary, consistently demonstrate that meaning and its particular sensuous embodiment cannot be dissociated, that "content" cannot be reduced to "information." Rainer Maria Rilke, that extraordinary poet of modernity, has eloquently shown us the impossibility of dissociating sex from love, one of the fundamental fallacies of our materialistic world view, and a fundamental prejudice underlying the devaluation of all poetic forms. It is only through seduction that we can enact compassion.

Over and beyond formal skills, however, there is the more subtle issue concerning the temporality involved in Holl's projects, the modes of experience proposed by his architecture. This issue could be summarized as the critical reinterpretation of the "program." Upon it hinges the possibility to transform a passive observer into a participant, allowing the inhabitant to recognize a potential wholeness through experience.

Indeed, how else can the work of architecture function as a setting-into-work of truth if not through this function of recognition/orientation? Plato spoke eloquently about our desire, throughout our mortal lives, to find "the other half" and complete the spheres that we once were. The space of architecture, always elusive and mysterious, is the space in which we may perceive ourselves, if only for a moment, as whole; it is the "event" (space/time) that may change our lives through this recognition. In *Timaeus,* Plato named this space "chora," the third element of reality (besides "Being" and "becoming"), encompassing both primordial space *and* matter. It is the "ground" of culture that can never be grasped directly either as an idea or through objectified sensation, but that nevertheless makes the miracle of language possible by relating the ideal (Being) to the concrete (becoming), and that only appears in works of human creation—as if in dreams.

This is the distant origin of Merleau-Ponty's reflection on intertwining. Architecture as intertwining thus hopes to present us with the wonder of depth as such (as the "first" dimension), appearing in a "thick" and reversible present, and to confront us with the mysterious origins of technology. Architectural space becomes a site of resistance against the collapse of desire that drives modernist technological utopias. The result is an architecture of dramatic situations whose subject matter is space/time—the *flesh* of the world. It engages our technological reality by its forms of expression in order to destructure the hegemony of use-values, and interworks perspectival, ocularocentric space in order to temporalize it.

Holl's struggle to engage these current philosophical reflections in the practice of architecture may be shunned by more pragmatic practitioners, yet it has a considerable lineage. This affinity with philosophy is part of our architectural tradition. Ever since Vitruvius, architects have endeavored to understand how architecture could function as a form of knowledge. The problem became more difficult at the beginning of the nineteenth century when architecture could no longer be understood as the representation of a socially shared cosmic picture. The question of how language, poetic and philosophical, relates to architectural practice is crucial, as it seems to hold a key for our understanding of architecture's potential relevance in the late twentieth century.

Following from Merleau-Ponty's insight in his late philosophy, phenomenological hermeneutics has recognized the *autonomy* of poetic language while demonstrating that its meaning hinges upon its capacity to speak about something "other" that "grounds" it and "precedes" it, even if this "other" is given *with* language. This would suggest the possibility of a politically appropriate, yet meaningful architecture, beyond the mystifications of egocentric formalism on one extreme, and the banalities of political correctness on the other; an architecture based on the recognition of the autonomy of its poetic language, while acknowledging the power of the individual imagination to make works that speak about *something*, and thus transcend irrelevant self-referential games.

For Holl, more specifically, the desire to engage Merleau-Ponty's late philosophy starts from a double awareness. On the one hand, the perception that architecture *matters*, that culture and architecture are inseparable and that their dissolution into the functional pragmatism of spaces for computer screens can only bring about a loss. On the other, an understanding that architecture cannot simply be identified with archaic forms of power or institutional presence and thus be "discarded" as a manifestation of the creative imagination. At stake is the very survival of architecture (and of human culture as we know it, that is, the space of desire) as the potential implementation of a more compassionate vision: an architecture driven by an ethical concern for the "other" rather than by aesthetic fashion, creating the possibility of meaning in diversity, rather than denoting *a* meaning.

Holl's most recent projects are the explorations along this road by a committed practitioner. Drawing from its philosophical affinities, his architecture does not pretend to refer back to absolute origins or foundations, and yet is equally unwilling to accept a simplistic relativism and the expression of cultural "difference" as its only options. It aspires to be architecture as an action, rather than a state of being, a discovery of order in making, which is also self-making, invoking a wholeness (and a holiness) that may stand for all in our compressed planet, and yet remain emphatically beyond tyranny and anarchy.

To what extent is it possible to engage the high stakes of late-capitalist culture in this mode of practice? Is it possible to build an architecture in the late-industrial city fully capable of acknowledging the *aporias* of time in our experience, history *and* the end of history, the quest for a better future *and* the end of progress, operating at a level "prior" to reductions, texts, and virtual reality? These are the questions that Holl addresses through his personal and imaginative, yet humble, work. His architecture refuses to choose between inhabiting a perpetual present (in which the weight of human actions is nullified and authorship does not matter) and a nonexistent point between past and future (in which human action is all that *is*, and authorship is infinitely glorified) in order to avoid logical contradictions. Responding to Merleau-Ponty's challenge, Steven Holl's work reinforces our hope in the possibility of a culturally significant architecture, a rare treat in a privatized world where the perception of reality is increasingly identified with a telematic "picture."

INTERTWINING

Steven Holl

Now, what kind of concept is this—the "intertwining?" It is, I suggest, a symbolical or metaphorical concept: a hermeneutic concept which comes from the inherent poetizing of radical phenomenological thinking. It is a concept genuinely grounded in our experience of the elemental, the primordial.

—David Michael Levin, *The Opening of Vision*

Architecture can shape a lived and sensed intertwining of space and time; it can change the way we live. Phenomenology concerns the study of essences; architecture has the potential to put essences back into existence. By weaving form, space, and light, architecture can elevate the experience of daily life through the various phenomena that emerge from specific sites, programs, and architectures. On one level, an idea-force drives architecture; on another, structure, material, space, color, light, and shadow intertwine in the fabrication of architecture. When we move through space with a twist and turn of the head, mysteries of gradually unfolding fields of overlapping perspectives are charged with a range of light—from the steep shadows of bright sun to the translucence of dusk. A range of smell, sound, and material—from hard stone and steel to the free billowing of silk—returns us to *primordial* experiences framing and penetrating our everyday lives.

Today architecture has the power to be both artistic and humanistic. This humanism fuses subjective and objective lives, intertwining inner and outer feelings, inner and outer thought, into a phenomena- inspired reformation of vision. It is the responsibility of every generation of architects to clarify a purpose—to articulate a vision through building. The present moment, infused with media imagery, is witness to surreal changes of multinational identities replacing the specificities of local cultures. The chaos and uncertainty of fluctuating economies, combined with an information overload from the ever-increasing supply of new technologies, contribute to a detachment from natural phenomena, thus giving rise to nihilistic attitudes. Architecture, with its silent spatiality and tactile materiality, can reintroduce essential, intrinsic meanings and values to human experience.

Consider a future humanism: an architecture that could be much more flexible in terms of the indeterminate and the acausal. Architecture could gain from the tremendous potential of information technologies as tools to assist in its concern for biological, social, and ecological issues. This approach, allowing self determination of social patterns in living spaces, would be distinct from mid-century modernism's positivistic, authoritarian determination. Our biological and ecological approach must develop more holistically; subjective and objective must intertwine.

Perception is Metaphorical

Perception of the every day—the joy of living with a vision open to phenomena—corresponds to a metaphorical experiencing of the world. David Michael Levin argues in fact that perception is spontaneously metaphorical. This perception is very different from a scientific observation or a rationalized vision. For example, early modern architects rationalized the use of light in buildings and called for the hygienic benefits of plate glass. Today, we also understand the importance of the subtleties and psychological differences of a vast range of qualities of light. With as much attention to darkness and to the contrasting secrets of light and dark, we engage in a metaphysics of light. Night's darkness evokes a connection to Dionysian archetypes and mysteries, while the bright light of day is Apollonian, exuberant, and unconcealed.

A metaphysics of light is part of intertwining essences with everyday materials, forms, and space. Concave windows cast a net of light ribbons on walls to trace the phenomena of glass as an ordinary material projecting and refracting extraordinary light. Diaphanous light reflecting on a still pond is a liquid, ghostly light. When a canoe paddle breaks the surface of water, a whorl is formed, a whirlpool mirror of light is sucked into the darkness. The nodal line ripples break vast water surfaces, dissipating into a flat curve.

The knowledge that the phenomena of space dimensions, time, and light are bound together in architecture is a wisdom of the ancients. The scholar and poet Rumi (1207–73) observed a special space from which "stars wheel around the North Pole." Likewise in the enormous timeless hollows of the Hagia Sophia in Istanbul rays of sculpted sunlight enter and rotate, animating the passing of time. Duration in light acts as the silent soul of that enormous space.

Enmeshing

Sitting by an old stone wall, a few moments past midday, one can see the sunlight, not quite perpendicular, catching all the stones that protrude and casting long shadows on the wall below. Where sunlight shines on irregular, convex stones, orange-brown and purple-gray hues are dramatically enhanced. In another instant, the sun passes and the wall is completely in shadow.

The merging of object and field yields an enmeshed experience, an interaction that is particular to architecture. Unlike painting or sculpture from which one can turn away, unlike music or film that one can turn off, architecture surrounds us. It promises intimate contact with shifting, changing, merging materials, textures, colors, and light in an intertwining of flat and deep three-dimensional parallactical space and time.

Architectural synthesis of changing background, middle ground, and foreground with all subjective qualities of material and light forms the basis for an intertwining perception. When we sit at a desk in a room by a window, the distant view, light from the window, material on the floor, wood on the desk, and the near eraser in hand all begin to merge. This overlap is crucial to the creation of an intertwining space. We must consider space, light, color, geometry, detail, and material in an intertwining continuum. Though we can disassemble these elements and study them individually during the design process, finally they merge. Ultimately, we cannot separate perception into geometries, activities, and sensations. Compressed, or sometimes expanded, the interlocking of light,

material, and detail creates over time a "whole" cinema of merging and yielding enmeshed experience.

Perpectival Space / Fluid Space

Proceeding through space in the city we move within a network of overlapping perspectives in motion. As the body advances, vistas open and close—distant, middle, and near views palpitate. The shifting movement between near and far objects, walls, and buildings makes an always-changing, visually tectonic landscape called "parallax." The promenade elicits a host of spontaneous intertwined experiences within urban space. In the complex spaces of the modern city, buildings are not so much objects as partial visions forming a perspectival continuum.

The horizon is porous, percolating with our movement, under construction, or eroding in time. At night solids and voids reverse themselves in a spatiality of darkness. A kaleidoscope of color, a misty night in New York is a

"There is no such thing as phenomenology, but there are indeed phenomenological problems."—Ludwig Wittgenstein

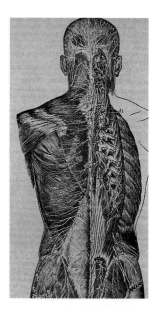

"Space brings the resonance of the acoustic near to life."—John Cage

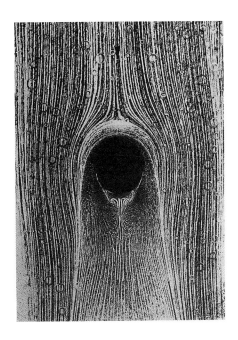

Laminar flow: movement around a cylinder

marvelous liquid matter of green beyond yellow; reddish ridges undulating on a blue haze; orange blurs slowly, unfolding from shapeless marks to precise white glows. The spaces, buildings, window walls, signs, and colors all intertwine. The glow of night's spatiality in the metropolis, a depth formed from shadows, colors, and a line of sight, differs from the depth of daytime spatiality formed by the sun.

Night light forms fluid luminous space. Fluid light has different viscosity—Tokyo night, Manhattan night, and Amsterdam night differ. The viscosity of night space has a density and a speed of flow particular to each specific place. Viscosity, the quality of gaseous or fluid bodies resulting from molecular attraction and density, determines the speed of flow. The different qualities of darkness and light affect not only a spatial, visual fluidity, but also a psychological·space of association—sometimes fast, other times slow. In a small town, for example, a glowing street lamp in the night rain makes a slowly moving viscous space. Architecture is sometimes only a slow viscosity of fluid space in motion.

Imagine in a building the difference in parallax experienced from overlapping perspectives be-

tween slipping, staggering, orthogonal spaces and curvilinear, bending, aqueous spaces. Spatial viscosity determines aqueous space. Architecture can define fluid movement by determining daytime and nighttime viscosities of light and shadow. Style and form at some point disappear—this is one metaphysics of intertwining.

Time is Duration
What are the facets of architecture's relationships with the fourth and fifth dimensions within a three-dimensional vocabulary? Time and perception in architecture intertwine with light and space of architecture within a certain duration. The philosopher Henri Bergson thought we should speak not of time, but of duration. The idea of lived time (*durée réelle*) is particular to each culture and has no universal definition. However, a useful framework of time's passage is discussed in *The Sacred and Profane* by Mircea Eliade. Eliade describes how two kinds of time, one a "succession of eternities," the other "an evanescent duration," exist for primitive man. In these early liturgical terms, calendar time flows in a closed circle, cosmic and sanctified by the gods. This conception of

time, akin to the cyclic time of Greek civilization, stands in extreme contrast to the Western view of ongoing historical time. Ongoing historical time's ever-shorter spans have become, in our media-conscious, sensationalist culture, especially tedious, and misleading.

The Greeks had a cosmological conception of time—a cosmic order that moves in a circle. Time had endlessness. This year Rosh Hashanah marks the celebration of the Jewish new year 5756. On spring equinox it will be the Persian new year of 1375. In four years, the so-called turn of the millennia brings the Western year 2000. Is our sense of time specific to the collective culture into which we are born? Or does our inner life—when it is strongly felt—assert a transcendent pull on inner time redoubling in a healthy skepticism? Perhaps we each have our own psychic field of time to challenge the unconscious acceptance of a pre-described, commercially driven time.

The reversibility of time, an idea discussed in recent modern physics, is a concept elaborated upon in ancient Buddhism. For the Buddhist, time consists of a continuous flux—a fluidity of time that makes every form that is manifest in

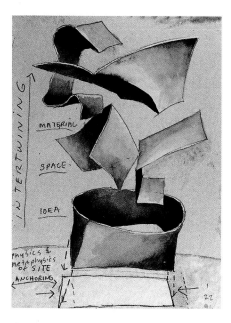

INTERTWINING

MATERIAL

SPACE

IDEA

physics &
metaphysics
of SITE

ANCHORING

22
91

"Words are his sails...the way they are set turns them into concepts."—Walter Benjamin, *Konvolut N*

time perishable. The instantaneity of time—another Buddhist concept—describes the unreality of the present instant which is continuously transformed into past and non-being.

The psychic field of time, the Buddhist's reversibility of time, and the instantaneity of time challenge the fixed time of architecture and advance a time of duration in architecture. Replacing Western time with Eastern time, we can extend the duration of architecture. This thinking together with sensory experience presents an architecture of continuous open flux—open to the distant past, wide open to a far away future that envelops the past, while the past envelops the future. Like a differential equation from integral calculus, a duration is described on an ascending, non-repeating cycle.

Time has long been posited as the fourth dimension of architecture, inseparable from its spaces. Erich Mendelsohn's Einstein Tower of 1919 built in Potsdam aimed at capturing dynamic mysteries of physics. The critic Robin Evans described its aspired space: "It required that space be conceived as a continuously altering field." Theo van Doesburg likewise aspired to space/time in his "Color Construction in the Fourth Dimension of Space-Time" of 1924.

Today, with Superstring theory, physicists speak of the fifth, sixth, and seventh dimensions.

**Gravity of Mass in Tension:
The Stone and The Feather**
The visionary Buckminster Fuller was a pioneer of the lightweight, the liberation of building from gravity. Fuller invented a conscious lightness. He fathered a weightlessness. He counterpoised heavy stone, brick and timber with the birdlike frame, the featherweight tensile skin. His systems of spider-weblike tensile domes and frames rejected the heavy for the light.

In contrast to such a singular, monistic philosophy, Italo Calvino mused in one of his last texts, *Six Memos for the Next Millennium*, "two opposite tendencies have competed in literature: one tries to make language into a weightless element that hovers above things like a cloud or perhaps the finest dust or better still a field of magnetic impulses. The other tries to give language the weight, density, and concreteness of things, bodies, and sensations." Calvino circumscribes a weightiness and the weightless as if they are two separate conditions, while in architecture one force—gravity—is inevitable.

A phenomenal architecture calls for both the stone and the feather. Sensed mass and perceived gravity directly affect our perceptions of architecture. The weight of the low, thick brick arches in Sigurd Lewerentz's Church at the Bottom of the Lake outside of Stockholm conveys the power of gravity and mass. Dim light gains its power from the heaviness of the brick masses overhead while also lighting the inner spaces. A duality exists in the bricks' weight pressing in on the dim light. The power and soul of this place would be erased if the space was built in lightweight metal construction.

Architecture's expression of mass and materials according to gravity, weight, bearing, tension, torsion, and buckling—like the orchestration of musical instruments—is made more dynamic through the contrast of heavy (bass, drums, tuba) and light (flute, violin, clarinet). The contrast in mass of the bass instruments in Béla Bartók's *Music for Strings Percussion and Celeste* is emphasized by the physical separation of the light and heavy instruments on stage during the performance of the piece. Music's materiality is resonantly conveyed via the instruments to aural temporal experience. Architecture's materiality is likewise conveyed via the structure and material of optic and haptic spatial experience.

Order, Geometry, Proportion

Order does not imply beauty.—Louis Kahn

City-order and nature-order exist in harmony and cacophony. As a stone spinning on a string exerts centrifugal force and the petals of a flower grow centrifugally, the geometry of the city and nature collide to form a tornado of centrifugal and/or centripetal forces. Such vortexes of city and nature signal other vortexes and geometries for intertwining with phenomena. On the molecular level the double helix structure of complementary (or homologous) chromosomes carries the genetic codes of heredity and reproduction. The work of intertwining considers new geometries and other orders, merging space and time in new ways.

The form of an architecture's geometry by itself is not univocal; its meaning is not fixed. In the abstract, no geometry is inferior to any other, none superior. Beginning with an infinite possibility of combinations of geometries (Euclidean, topological, Boolean), as well as the open possibility of any syntactical logic of architecture, possible expressions are infinite. And yet the idea-force that drives an architectural design, the idea that wraps manifold factors and elements in a whole expression, is finite. Geometrical infinities are constantly subjected to finite ideas.

Idea / Limit

Architecture transcends geometry. It is an organic link between concept and form. Architecture's meaning lies in the intertwining of its site, its phenomena, its idea. Architecture may be expressive, yet it also carries like a vehicle ontological and epistemological maps. Site-force, circumstance, program, and phenomena are connected with idea-force. Forming a concept defines a field of inquiry—a territory of research for investigation that helps to form meaning. The idea is the force that drives the design. The field of inquiry sets the focus and the limit and, most importantly, the responsibility of work in rigor and depth.

What is an excellent concept? How can we interpret its strength or weakness? A manifold relation of complex elements are held together by a concept. A concept's distinctness and clarity is limited to a situation and can build meaning into a site and program. The organizing idea is a hidden thread connecting disparate parts with exact intention. Organizing ideas are heuristic devices that can tie disparate architectural elements into a larger whole, and yet they must be free and open enough for functional development. As heuristic devices, they can be invented from inspirations of site history, program, or geography. As mytho-poetic stories, buildings make connections to histories, sites, cultures, and passions.

Material and the Haptic Realm

One sees the hardness and brittleness of glass and when, with a tinkling sound, it breaks, this sound is conveyed by the visible glass. One sees the springiness of steel, the ductility of red-hot steel, the hardness of a plane blade, the softness of shavings.—Maurice Merleau-Ponty, *Phenomenology of Perception*

Church at Borgund, central Norway (remains unchanged since middle ages). Entering the blackened building, the smell of tar on wood is the most powerful sensation. . . until the eyes gradually adjust to the dim light.

The experience of material in architecture is not just visual but tactile, aural, olfactory; it is all of these intertwined with space and our bodily trajectory in time. Perhaps no other realm more directly engages multiple phenomena and sensory experience than the haptic realm.

The haptic realm of architecture is defined by the sense of touch. When the materiality of the details forming an architectural space become evident, the haptic realm opens up. Sensory experience is intensified, psychological dimensions engaged.

Today the industrial and commercial forces at work on the "products" for architecture tend toward the synthetic; wooden casement windows are delivered with weatherproof plastic vinyl coverings, metals are "anodized" or coated with a synthetic outer finish, tiles are glazed with colored synthetic coatings, and stone is simulated, as is wood grain. The sense of touch is dulled or canceled with these commercial industrial methods. The texture and essence of material and detail is displaced.

Materials may be altered through a variety of means that do not diminish, and may even enhance, their natural properties. Glass becomes radiant as, in transformed states, its functional role is shifted. Bending glass induces dazzling variations to a simple plane with the geometric curvature of reflected light. Cast glass with its mysterious opacity traps light in its mass and projects it in a diffused glow. Sand-blasted glass, likewise, has a luminescence that changes subtly, depending on the glass thickness and type and the grain size of the silica sand used.

Metals can be significantly transformed by sandblasting, bending, and acid oxidization to create rich materiality of surface and color. The beauty of various colors and textures of oxida-tion, integral to materials and their weathering change in time, give details a time-colored dimension. Cast metals, aluminum, bronze, and brass add to the palette of alternatives. A variety of metals, such as copper, nickel, and zinc, can now be electronically atomized, and sprayed nearly cold in a layer over a surface of a different material, opening up new possibilities for finished and plastic details.

The texture of a silk drape, the sharp corners of cut steel, the mottled shade and shadow of rough sprayed plaster, and the sound of a spoon striking a concave wooden bowl reveal an authentic essence that stimulates the senses.

Remaining Experimental

In Spinoza's thought, life is not an idea, a matter of theory. It is a way of being....Spinoza did not believe in hope or even in courage; he believed in joy, and in vision.—Gilles Deleuze, *Expression in Philosophy*

Architecture must remain experimental and open to new ideas and aspirations. In the face of tremendous conservative forces that constantly push it towards the already proven, already built, and already thought, architecture must explore the not-yet felt. Only in an aspiring mode can the visions of our lives be concretized and the joy shared with future generations.

If a project's program is destitute it is the architect's responsibility to invent and attempt new programs. Rather than simply solving for a given program, what architecture contributes beyond the program is important. A failure of nerve today represents the collapse of a profession and the withdrawal of an art. We must remain open and experimental and, perhaps, marginal. The realization of one inspired idea in turn inspires others. Phenomenal experience, worth the fight, is answered without words—the silent response is the joy radiated in the light space and materials of architecture.

With *Intertwining* we begin a new chapter of *Anchoring* where the site/situation is both subject and object, both existence and essence. A new intensity is anticipated in a criss-crossing of the tangible (haptic), the thought (idea-force), and the site. In the intertwining of idea-force, phenomenal properties, and site-force, three do not quite merge into one. Herein lies a mystery that is familiar but unexplained. The intertwining has a "between" that alternates from within to without. Our body moves through and, simultaneously, is coupled with the substances of architectural space—the "flesh of the world." (Maurice Merleau-Ponty)

This paradox of the seer and the seen is a reflexivity of touch-vision that includes thought. In a three-dimensional triad, the reciprocal insertion of the body—oneself—in the inter-woven landscapes of architecture yields identity and difference. This insertion of oneself is an intertwining of one in the other of architecture. Without purpose as an object, without recourse as a style, architecture depends on this reciprocal insertion of the other, oneself. From this unique position, fresh experiences avail themselves. The body concentrates the mysteries.

Within this fresh chiasma of a phenomenal architecture, our aim is to explore the not-yet-worked-over. The aim for a vision that begins in the particularity of site and is culturally grounded is propelled by idea toward the touch-vision axis and toward phenomenal experience. Not only an architecture of feeling, our aim is for an intertwining of subjective-objective. Our aim is to realize space with strong phenomenal properties while elevating architecture to a level of thought.

SELECTED

PROJECTS

1 9 8 9 – 1 9 9 5

Void Space / Hinged Space Housing
Fukuoka, Japan, 1989–91

Four quiet south-facing voids interlock with four active north-facing voids to bring a sense of the sacred into direct contact with everyday domestic life. To ensure emptiness, the south voids are flooded with water; the sun reflects off them, flickering across the ceilings of the north courts and the apartments.

Interiors of the twenty-eight apartments revolve around the concept of "hinged space," a development of the multi-use concepts of traditional *fusuma* taken into an entirely modern dimension. Diurnal hinging allows an expansion of the living area during the day and a reclamation of bedrooms at night. Episodic hinging reflects the change in a family over time: rooms can be added or subtracted to accommodate grown-up children leaving the family or elderly parents moving in.

The experience of passing through space is heightened in the three types of access, which allow all apartments to have exterior front doors. On the lower passage, views across the water court and through the north voids activate the walk spatially from side to side. Along the north passage, with a view of the park in the distance, one has a sense of suspension. The top passage has a sky view under direct sunlight.

The apartments interlock in section like a complex Chinese box. Aiming for individuation, every apartment is different. Due to the voids and interlocking sections, each apartment has north, south, east, and west exposures.

The structure of exposed bearing concrete is stained in some places. A lightweight aluminum curtain wall allows a reading of the building sections while walking from east to west along the street; an entirely different facade of solids is exposed walking from west to east.

The building, with its street-aligned shops and intentionally simple facades, is seen as part of a city in its effort to form space rather than become an architecture of object. Space is its medium, from active urban space to private hinged space.

When we revisited the totally inhabited building in 1992 the residents had formed themselves into a community group and held sake parties every month on the roof. They had all met showing each other the differences in their apartments.

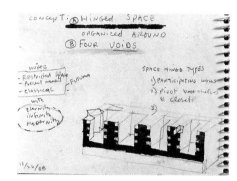

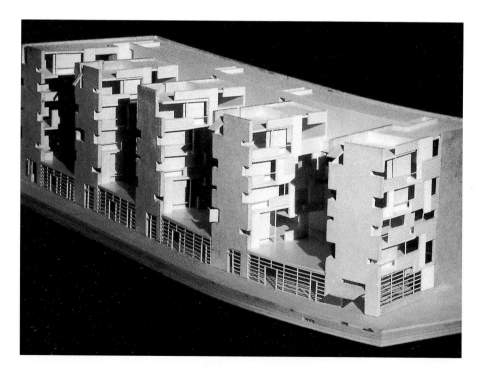

Site plan
Left: Steven Holl
Center: Rem Koolhaas
Right: Mark Mack

Four paired voids
Housing units are arranged around four south-facing courts, void spaces within the domestic block. Flooded with water, these are meditative spaces held apart from day-to-day activities. Corresponding to each is a sheltered court to the north. These spaces are set aside as play areas for children and seating for a ground-floor cafe; they face onto a common garden. Each pair is joined together by a large opening and a flight of steps. Light from the water court spills into the paved court; in return, the sounds of children playing and of conversation percolate into the meditative space. The apposition of phenomena corresponds to the sheared section of the voids.

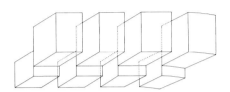 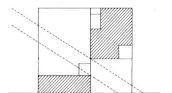

Proportion
All major dimensions in plan and section correspond to a proportional series (1:1.618) based on the width of the court spaces.

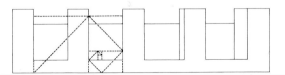

Structure
Concrete bearing walls with secondary columns at midslab. West elevations of the courts are infill curtain walls; east elevations are concrete bearing walls. To the passerby headed west the composition of the building is planar; to one headed east the building appears volumetric.

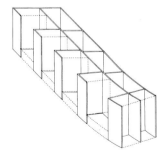 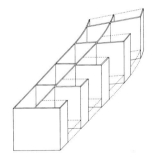

Passages between voids
Public walkways provide access to the housing units and connect the void courts. The space along each passage develops a different spatial relation: inside or beside the court, directed to the city, the park, or the sky.

 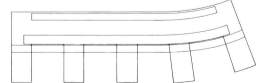

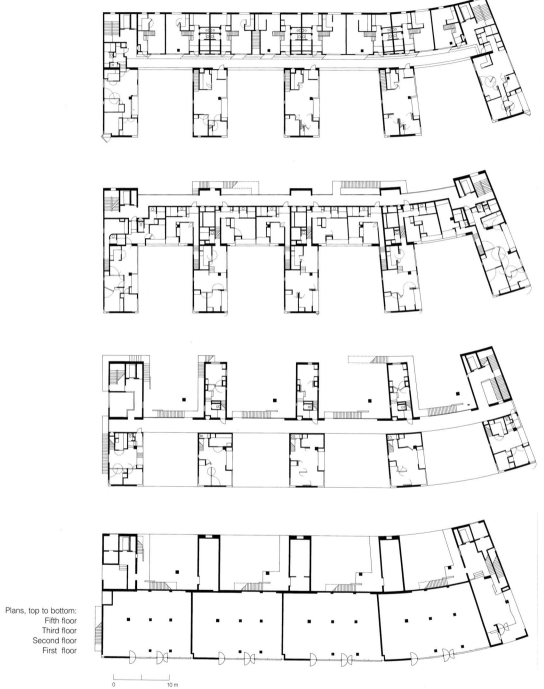

Plans, top to bottom:
Fifth floor
Third floor
Second floor
First floor

0   10 m

Spatial extension
The one-directional courts relieve the
compactness of the housing units in a
way that is analogous to the traditional
walled garden of domestic spaces.

Hinged space
By using pivoting doors, panels, and
cabinets, the plan of each unit can be
reconfigured to accommodate diurnal
and episodic changes.

Left: Section at void spaces
Center: Section at open void
Bottom: Section at second-floor access

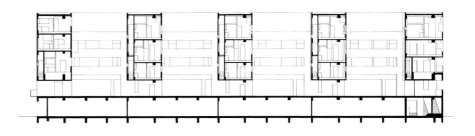

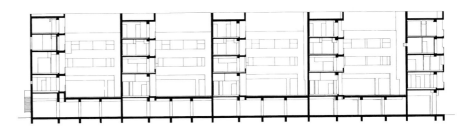

Unit types
The 28 apartment units are divided into 18 variants of 5 types: "L" (*L*-shaped plan), "I" (*I*-shaped plan), "D" (double level), and the combinations "DL" and "DI." Units interlock in plan and in section, interconnecting the different court spaces. Each apartment is different; all have at least three exposures.

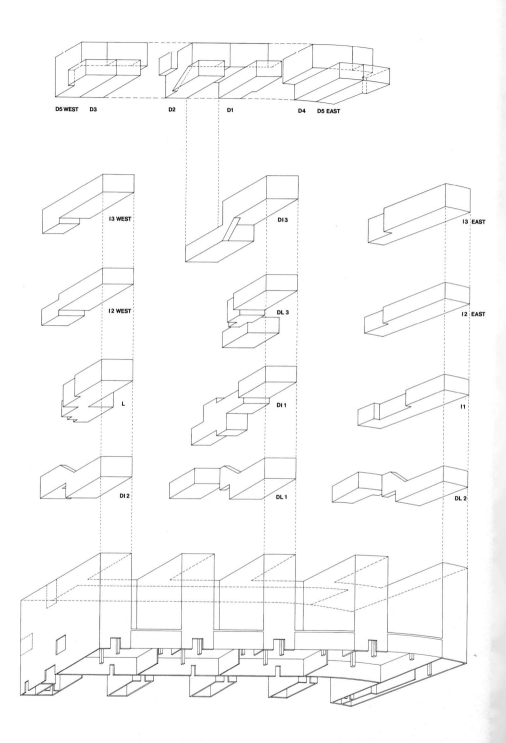

D5 WEST   D3   D2   D1   D4   D5 EAST

I3 WEST   DI3   I3 EAST

I2 WEST   DL 3   I2 EAST

L   DI 1   I1

DI 2   DL 1   DL 2

The north courts are the void inversions
of the watercourts in the south

The watercourt, like a phenomenal
lens, brings the sky, the clouds, and
the rain into the heart of the building

Right: Second-floor walkway, the
end of the overlapping perspective
is concealed in the curve

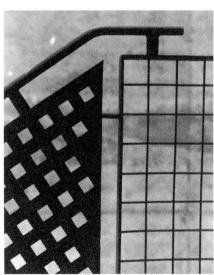

Multiple use of small apartments with hinged space. Diurnal change allows expansion of the living area during the day. Episodic change allows rooms to be subtracted when grown-up children leave the house or added when the elderly move in.

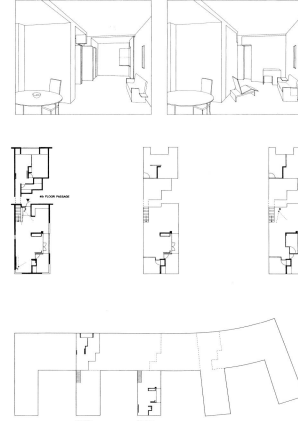

4th. FLOOR PASSAGE

4th. FLOOR   5th. FLOOR

Hinged space
Top: Closed
Bottom: Open

28

Hinged space
Top: Closed
Bottom: Open
Right: Resident demonstrating
hinged panel

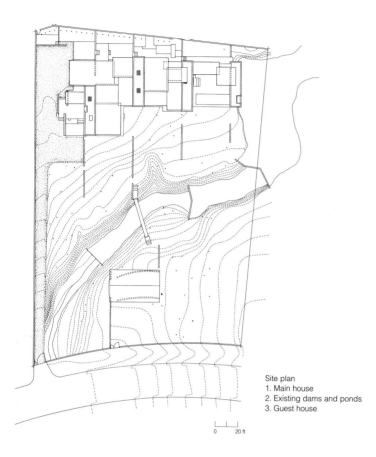

Site plan
1. Main house
2. Existing dams and ponds
3. Guest house

0   20 ft

Stretto House
Dallas, Texas, 1989–91

Sited adjacent to three spring-fed ponds with existing concrete dams, the house projects the character of the site in a series of concrete block "spatial dams" with a metal-framed "aqueous space" flowing through them. Coursing over the dams, like the overlapping stretto in music, water provides an overlapping reflection of the space of the landscape outside as well as the virtual overlapping of the spaces inside.

A particular composition using this stretto, Béla Bartók's *Music for Strings, Percussion and Celeste*, was paralleled in the form of the house. The piece's four movements have a distinct division between heavy (percussion) and light (strings). Whereas music has a materiality in instrumentation and sound, this architecture attempts an analogue in light and space, that is,

$$\frac{material \times sound}{time} = \frac{material \times light}{space}$$

The building is formed in four sections, each consisting of two modes: heavy orthogonal masonry and light and curvilinear metal. The concrete block and metal structures recall the Texas vernacular. The plan is purely orthogonal, while the section is curvilinear. The guest house is an inversion with the plan curvilinear and section orthogonal, similar to the inversions of the subject in the first movement of the Bartók score. In the main house aqueous space is developed by several means: floor planes pull the level of one space through to the next, roof planes pull space over walls, and an arched wall pulls light down from a skylight. Materials and details continue the spatial concepts in poured concrete, glass cast in fluid shapes, slumped glass, and liquid terrazzo.

Arriving at the building via a driveway bridging over a stream, a visitor passes through overlapping spaces of the house, glimpsing the flanking gardens, and arrives at an empty flooded room. The room, doubling its space in reflection, opening both to the site and the house, becomes the asymmetrical center of two sequences of aqueous space.

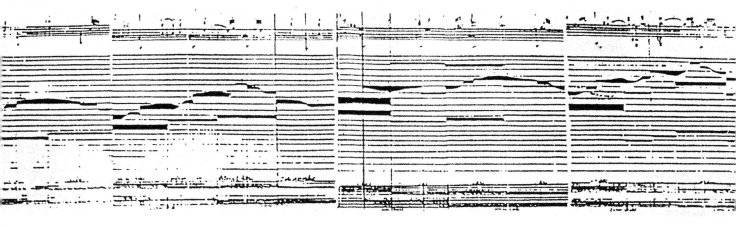

Paul Klee's analysis of a musical score

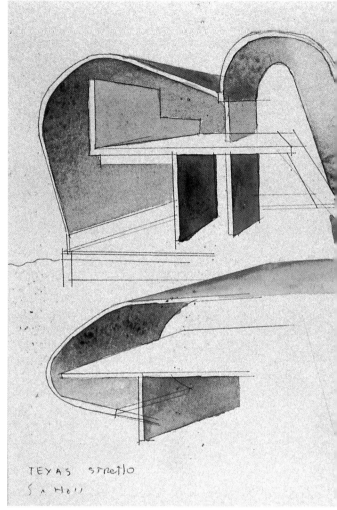

TEYAS STRETTO
S. Holl

Far left and above: Concept sketche
Left: Existing spring-fed ponds

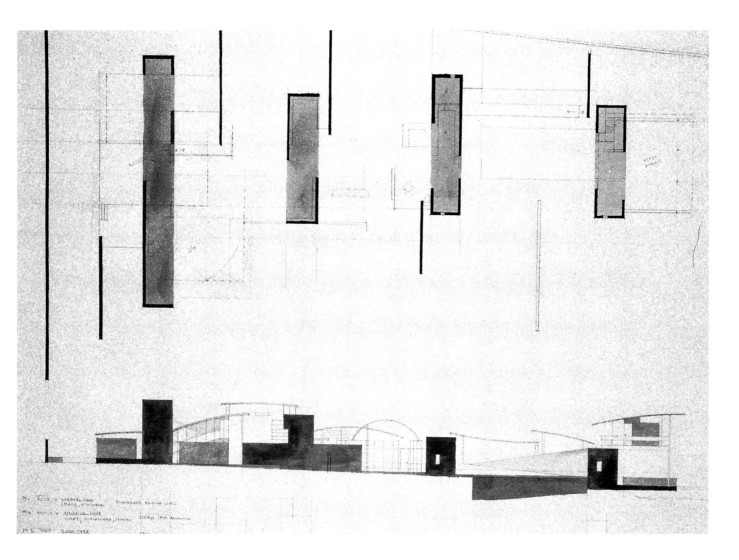

Like Bartók's *Music for Strings, Percussion and Celeste*, the house is divided into four movements, alternating heavy and light

East elevation

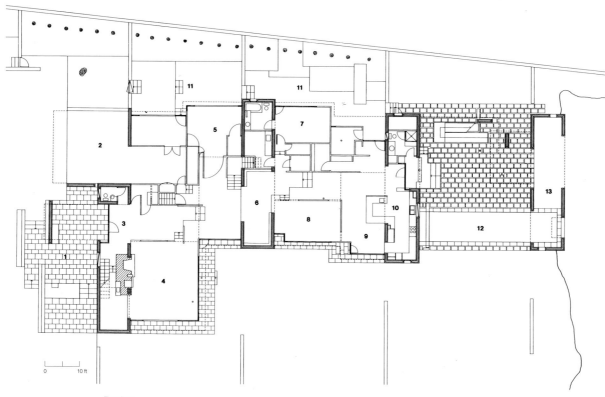

First floor
1. Terrace
2. Garage
3. Entry
4. Living room
5. Art storage supply
6. Library
7. Study
8. Dining room
9. Breakfast area
10. Kitchen
11. Walled garden
12. Pool
13. Flooded room

0   10 ft

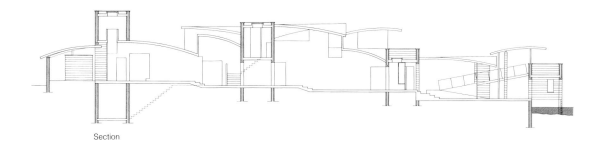

Section

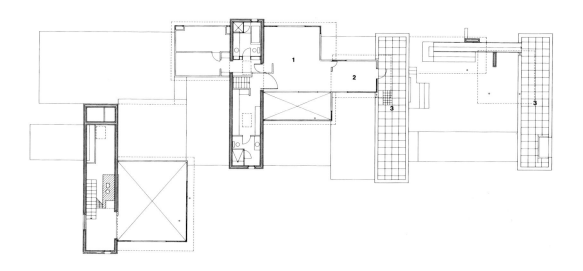

Second floor
1. Bedroom
2. Sitting room
3. Roof terrace

Facing page: Exploded axonometric
Right: View from interior
Below: Steel tube lightweight "bones" braced
against masonry heavyweight structure

Left: Exterior view toward living room
Below: Front entrance

Fluidity of terrazzo at each spatial dam

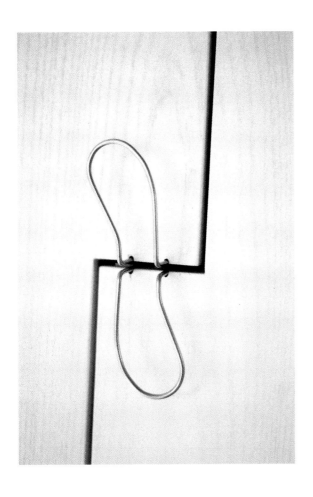

Facing page: Cast glass fountain as a
melting slab of ice at entry
Left: A greasy finger hooks the cabinet...
without leaving a mark
Below: Curved window in art library

Guest House: the architectural correlative to the "retrograde row" in music (the measure played backward and upside down), the guest house is the geometric inverse of the house

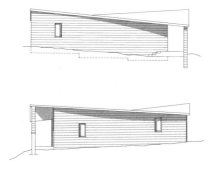

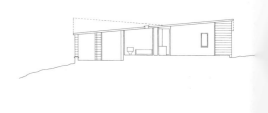

Above: Overview of project
Right: Detail of flooded room

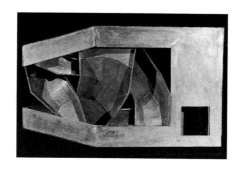

Palazzo del Cinema
Venice, Italy, 1990

For a competition for the Venice Film Festival Building the connection from Venice to the Lido site by water is emphasized by a grand arrival of space on the lagoon. Filled with diaphanous light from gaps between the cinemas above, this space—a homage to Venice—would also be a place for the Lido community. During the months when there is no cinema festival, this public grotto might have shops along the arcade or marina functions coexisting with the Palazzo del Cinema.

Time in its various abstractions links architecture and cinema. The project involves three interpretations of time and light in space. Collapsed time and extended time within cinema—the ability to depict twenty years in one minute or four seconds in twenty minutes—is expressed in the warp and extended weave of the building. Diaphanous time is reflected in sunlight dropping through fissures between the cinemas into the lagoon basin below. Ripples of water and reflected sunlight animate the grand public grotto. Absolute time is measured in a projected beam of sunlight that moves across the "cubic Pantheon."

The projection of light in space, in reflection, and in shade and shadow are seen as programmatic aspects to be achieved parallel to solving functional aspects. A vessel for "filmic time" and "filmic space," the building has a bottle-shaped perimeter with the mouth open to the lagoon towards Venice. The cinemas interlock within this frame, creating crevices that allow sunlight to the water below. In section the cinemas turn slightly, like interlocking hands, changing their interior and exterior aspects of space.

The lobby at the end of the covered boat basin opens to the east and the west. Escalators take people to the upper level lobby, which has a cafe and a view toward the horizon of the Adriatic. The escalators pass through the lobby space in sections like the weave of theaters over the lagoon. The main facade of cable-reinforced sand-blasted acrylic responds to this warp and weave.

The main structure is of planar concrete. Metal formwork for the concrete is retained on the exterior face. Made of a brass alloy, this metal acquires a red patina. When the festival opens the cinema screens can be rolled up, and the cinema images projected onto warped concrete planes that interrupt the monolithic red patina of the exterior. Film is then projected through the folds and warps in the holes; with dissected colors and light architecture chops up cinema. Here cinema burns holes in architecture.

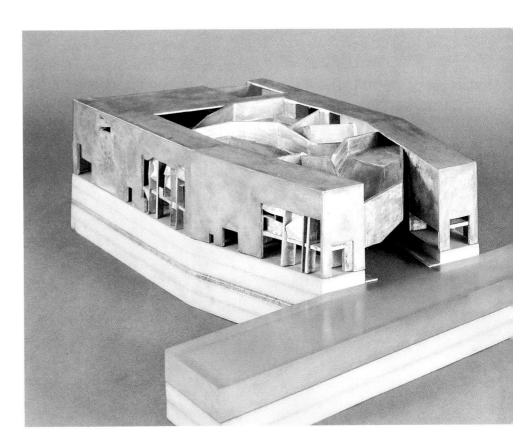

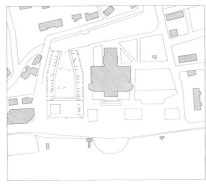

Left: Grottoes on the lagoon
Above: Site plan
1. Existing lagoon
2. New public grottoes
3. Adriatic Sea

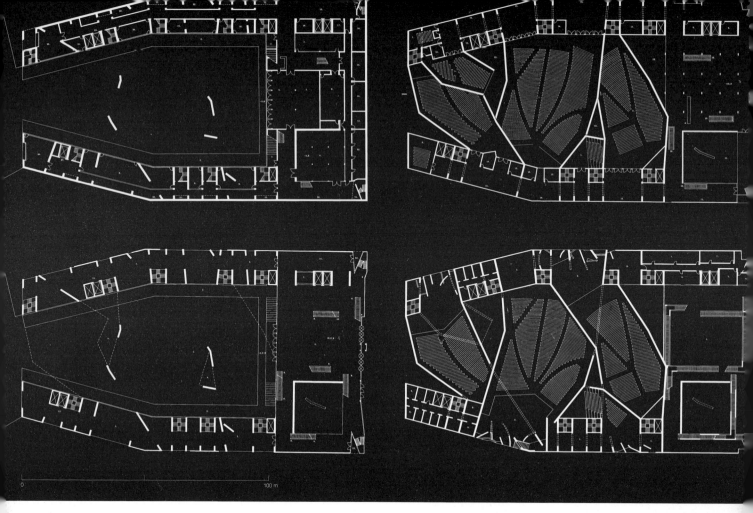

Bottom left: Ground level
1. Covered boat basin
2. Boat landing
3. Arcade
4. Fissure above
5. Special reception—"cubic Pantheon"
6. Main lobby
7. Ticket window
8. Escalator
9. Stair to press offices
10. Stair to offices, washrooms
11. Telephone area
12. Glass pavers
13. Service elevator

Top left: Basin level
1. Covered boat basin
2. Boat landing
3. Stair to main lobby
4. Journalists' writing room
5. Editors' room
6. Journalists' communications
7. Offices
8. Conference room / TV studio
9. Press boxes
10. Photocopy room
11. Glass pavers above
12. Darkroom
13. First aid room
14. Dressing rooms
15. Exhibit hall
16. Public washrooms
17. Mechanical room
18. Hospitality office
19. Bookshop
20. Supply office
21. Technical activities office
22. Storeroom
23. Service elevator
24. Mechanical room

Bottom right: Intermediate level 1
1. Cinema 1 for 1600 people
2. Cinema 2 for 1200 people
3. Cinema 3 for 700 people
4. Cinema 4 for 200 people
5. Cinema 5 for 100 people
6. Escalator
7. Fissure
8. Stage
9. Backstage / storage
10. Director's office
11. General secretarial office
12. Administrative services
13. Payroll department
14. Washroom
15. Switchboard, postal services
16. Personnel room
17. Jury room
18. Custodian's lodging

Top right: Cinema entry level
1. Cinema 1 for 1600 people
2. Cinema 2 for 1200 people
3. Cinema 3 for 700 people
4. Cinema 4 for 200 people
5. Cinema 5 for 100 people
6. Cinema 6 for 60 people
7. Cinema 7 for 40 people
8. Upper lobby / restaurant
9. Kitchen
10. Escalator
11. Terrace
12. Fissure
13. Rest room / utility room
14. Translation cabin
15. Coat check
16. Bar

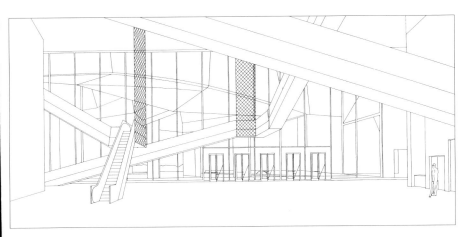

Left top: Section A-A
1. Covered boat basin
2. Boat landing
3. Arcade
4. Cinema 3
5. Cinema 4
6. Stage
7. Backstage and storage
8. Offices
9. Circulation

Left bottom: Section B-B
1. Covered boat basin
2. Boat landing
3. Arcade
4. Cinema 1
5. Cinema 2
6. Cinema 5
7. Stage
8. Backstage and storage
9. Offices
10. Circulation

Right: Section C-C
1. Cinema 1
2. Cinema 2
3. Cinema 3
4. Cinema 4
5. Covered boat basin
6. Boat landing
7. Main lobby
8. Upper lobby
9. Press offices
10. Press writing room

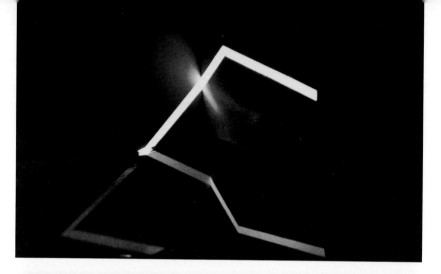

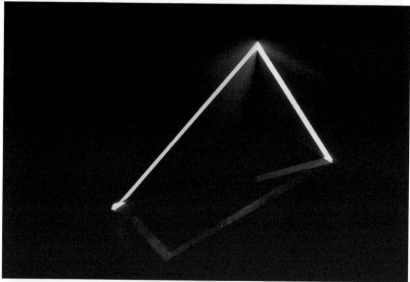

Three times of day in a cubic Pantheon
of absolute time, adjacent to the lobby

Right: East elevation, early study
Below: Watercolor view from Lido

Edge of a City
1988–90

The health of the eye seems to demand a horizon.
We are never tired so long as we can see far enough.
—Ralph Waldo Emerson

On the fringe of today's modern city, displaced fragments sprout without intrinsic relationships to existing organization, other than that of the camber and loops of the curvilinear freeway. Here the discarded spreads itself outward like the nodal lines of a stone tossed into a pond. The edge of a city is a philosophical region, where city and natural landscape overlap, existing without choice or expectation.

This zone calls for visions and projections to delineate the boundary between the urban and the rural. Visions of a city's future can be plotted on this partially spoiled land, liberating the remaining natural landscape, protecting the habitat of hundreds of species of animals and plants that are threatened with extinction. What remains of the wilderness can be preserved; defoliated territory can be restored. In the middle zone between landscape and city, there is hope for a new synthesis of urban life and urban form. Traditional planning methods are no longer adequate. Looking back at the city from the point of view of the landscape, these projects consider untested programs and new kinds of urban spaces.

The exploration of strategies to counter sprawl at the periphery of cities—the formation of spaces rather than the formation of objects—are primary aims of the Edge of a City projects. The expanded boundary of the contemporary city calls for the synthesis of new spatial compositions. An intensified urban realm could be a coherent mediator between the extremes of the metropolis and the agrarian plan.

In each proposal, living, working, recreational, and cultural facilities are juxtaposed in new pedestrian sectors that might act as social condensers for new communities. From "spatial retaining bars" that protect the desert at the edge of Phoenix, Arizona to the parallax towers that frame the view of the urban landscape in New York City, these plans intertwine with existing circumstances. Though they differ in form, these proposals share a pre-theoretical ground of psychological space, program, movement, light quality, and tactility.

Stitch Plan
Cleveland, Ohio, 1989

Five Xs spaced along the inland edge of
Cleveland (the northern edge is formed by Lake
Erie) define precise crossover points from new
urban areas to clarified rural regions. These
newly created urban spaces are girded by
mixed-use buildings. Taken together, the Xs
imply an urban edge.

At one X the crossover is developed into
a dam with hybrid functions. Here the urban
section contains a number of buildings
including a hotel, a cinema, and a gymnasium.
The rural section contains public programs
related to nature, including a fish hatchery, an
aquarium, and botanical gardens. The artificial
lake formed by the dam provides a recreational
area and extends the crossover point into a
boundary line.

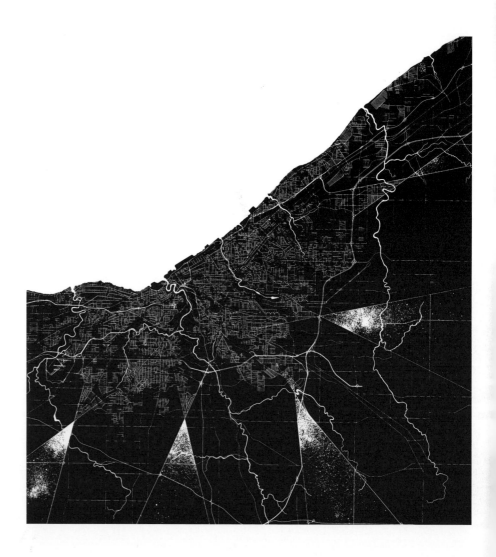

Right: Cleveland site map with "stitches"
Facing page: Cleveland horizon with X

Left: Model of hybrid dam
Facing page: Axonometric of hybrid dam, site plan, and building section

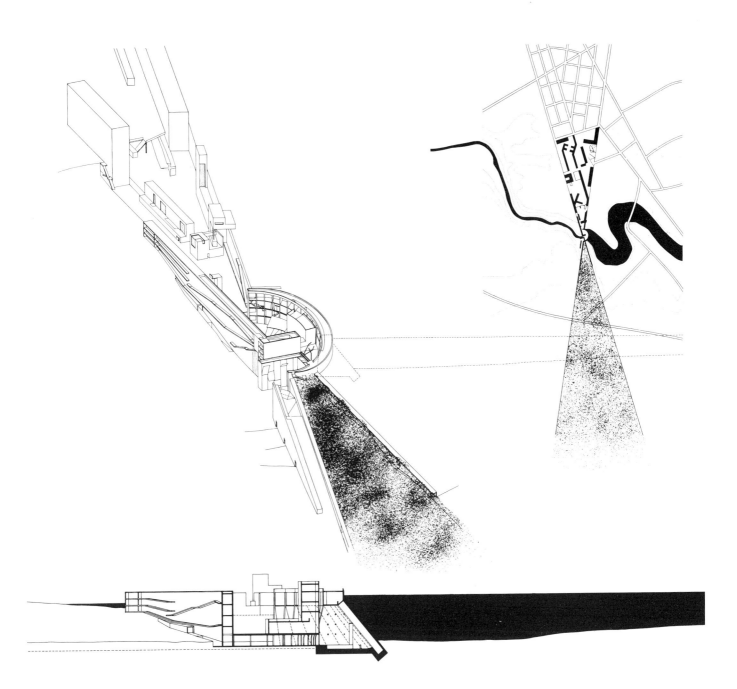

Above: Phoenix at night
Right: Phoenix map with
spatial retaining bars

Spatial Retaining Bars
Phoenix, Arizona, 1989

The mysterious disappearance of the Hohokum
civilization after 1000 years of continuous
cultivation of the valley of the Gila and Salt
rivers is a prominent aspect of the history of
Phoenix. Sited on this land on the periphery of
Phoenix, a series of spatial retaining bars infer
an edge to the city and a beginning to the
desert. Each structure inscribes a space and
rises to frame views of the distant mountains
and desert.

The loftlike living areas in the upper arms of
the bars hang in silent isolation and form a new
horizon with views of the desert sunrise and
sunset. Courtyards at grade provide entrance
to and exit from the buildings and encourage a
sense of community. Work is conducted electronically from loft-spaces adjoining dwellings.
Cultural facilities are suspended in open frame
structures.

The thirty-foot-square building sections act as
reinforced concrete hollow beams. Exteriors are
of pigmented concrete. The undersides of the
arms are polished to a high gloss. In the morning and evening they are illuminated by the red
desert sun—a hanging apparition of light once
reflected by the water of the 250 miles of thirty-
foot Hohokum canals.

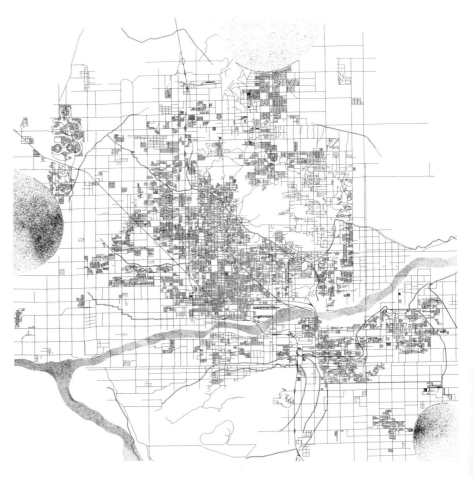

Left: Composite of spatial
retaining bars at site
Below: Detail

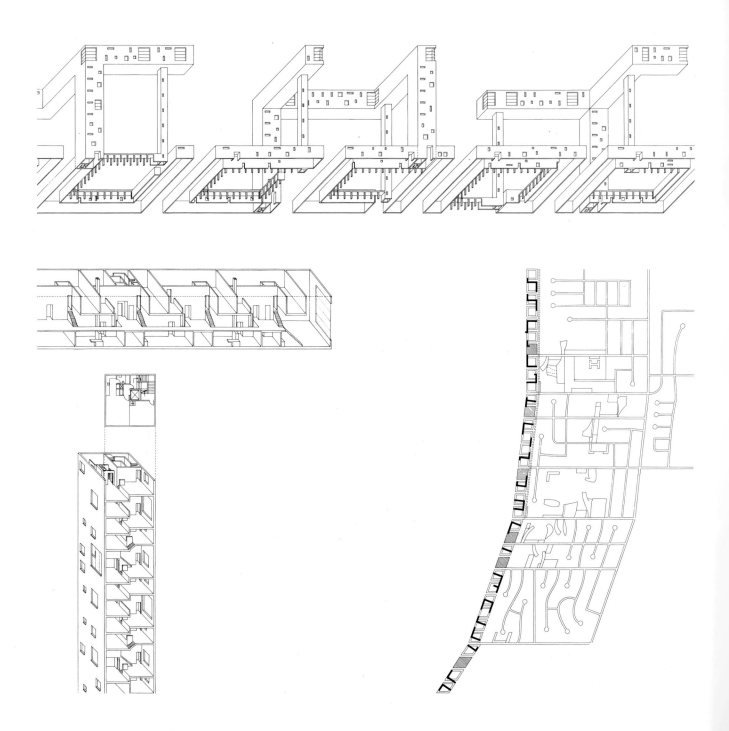

Facing page: Plan, interior axonometric, and worm's-eye view
Right: Section model of courtyard building
Left: Model of spatial retaining bars

ERIE CANAL

Erie Canal Edge
Rochester, New York, 1988

The Erie Canal, a grand work that secured the growth of New York and of cities along its route, is now an undistinguished trench to the south of Rochester. This project is a cross-sectional study that redefines the canal and reinforces the city edge.

Canal-house types rest on the top and bottom of the canal's embankment, like dogs at the dinner table. On the north side of the canal, the houses form a continuous wall and an intermittent arcade; on the south, they are misaligned and open to the rural areas beyond.

The northern urban edge contains a workplace building that anticipates new programs not requiring horizontal floors. Operation occurs via walkway beams analogous to the former work walks along the Erie Canal.

Between the work building and the canal houses are a series of social and cultural facilities: a group of cinemas, a music school, and housing for the elderly with a connecting gallery.

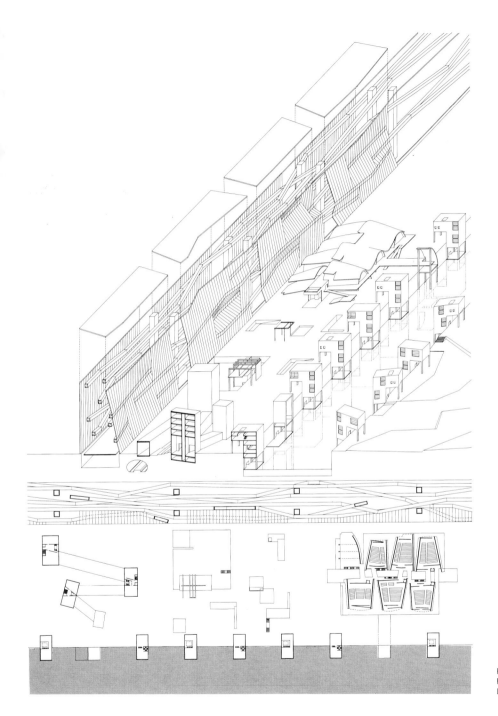

Facing page top: Rochester site plan
Facing page bottom: Existing canal
Left: Axonometric, plan, and section

Above and facing page top:
Model view, canal house types in foreground
Facing page bottom: Model view of cinema building

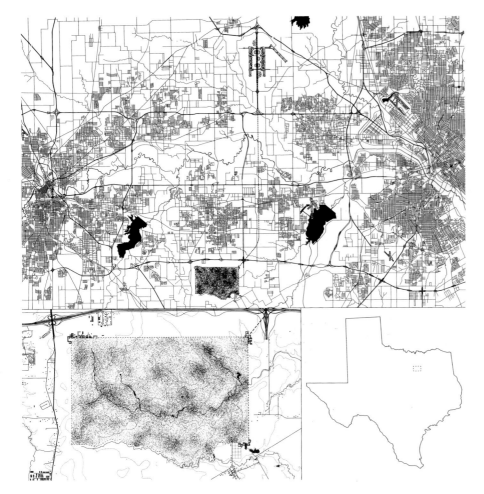

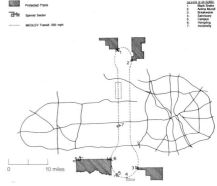

Left: Dallas / Fort Worth site plan
Above: Spiroid sector site diagram
Facing page: Photomontage of model in site

Spiroid Sectors
Dallas / Fort Worth, Texas, 1990

This proposal for a new hybrid building type is
sited in the partly settled area between Dallas
and Fort Worth. Protected Texas prairie is
framed by new sectors condensing living,
working, and recreation activities. Inhabitants
are delivered auto-free by high-speed MEGLEV
transit from the Dallas / Fort Worth Airport in
minutes.

A new hierarchy of public spaces is framed
by the armatures that are knotted in a continuous "holding together" morphology. Various
public passages along the roof afford a shifting
ground plane, thus invigorating the interconnected experience of the sector's spaces.

The looping armatures contain a hybrid of
macro programs—public transit stations, health
clubs, cinemas, and galleries—with horizontal
and vertical interconnected transit. Micro-
programs of domestic activities are contained in
smaller adjacent structures. The smallest
spiroids form low-cost courtyard housing in
experimental planar wall construction that varies
between thin and thick.

Above: Pure planar construction,
exploded axonometric
Right: Large spiroid model with
beam of pure planar construction;
installation, Walker Art Center,
Minneapolis, 1991

Above: Provisional housing model
within large spiroid construction
Right: Provisional housing plan

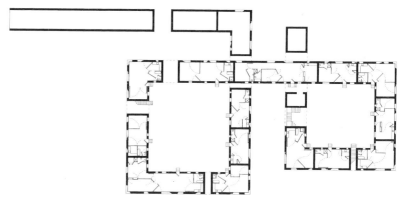

Right: Institute of Science, plate tectonics, and tornado machine
Facing page: MAGLEV station, public spaces, and cinema

Parallax Towers
New York, New York, 1990

In this proposal, the existing 72nd Street train yards would be transformed into a new city-edge park in the spirit of Frederick Law Olmsted's work. The existing dense development to the east looks out over this new open park, which extends to the Hudson River's edge.

On the river, ultrathin skyscrapers bracket the view and create a new kind of framed urban space over water. Hybrid buildings with diverse functions, the towers are linked by horizontal underwater transit systems that connect underwater parkside lobbies to high-speed elevators serving upper transfer lobbies. Occupants are within walking distance of the 72nd Street subway entrance or express ferries to the Jacob K. Javits Convention Center, Wall Street, and LaGuardia Airport.

In counterbalance to the ultrathin towers, an ultra-thick floating public space is used as a concert stadium, large-screen movie theater complex, or grand festival hall.

Right: Model of parallax towers
Facing page: Site plan

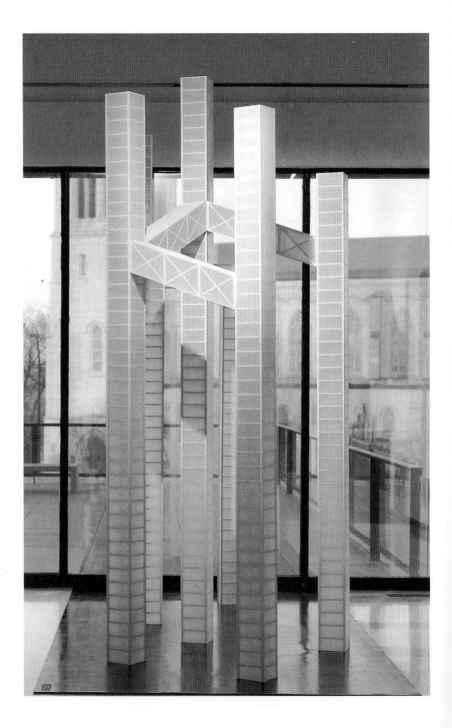

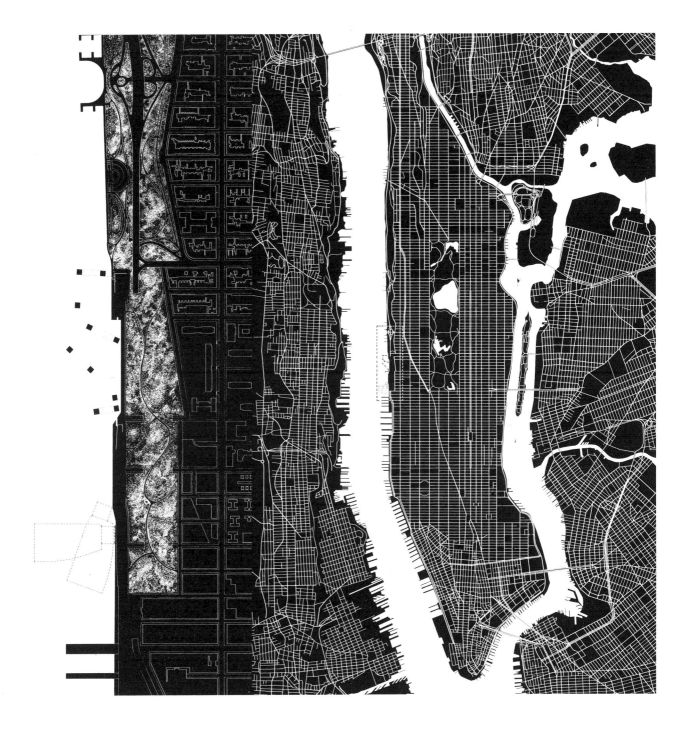

D. E. Shaw & Company Offices
New York, New York, 1991

The top two floors of a midtown Manhattan skyscraper are the site of a project exploring the phenomena of spatial color reflection or projected color.

D. E. Shaw & Company, a financial trading firm, works with the miniscule drift of prices from stock trading measured over short intervals of time. The firm's computers are connected to financial markets by satellite and by telephone lines and rest only between the time the Tokyo exchange has closed and the London exchange has opened. One room in the facility contains more than 200 small computers.

This curious and intangible business program is paralleled in the design of the interior. The metal framing and Sheetrock with skimcoat plaster was carved and notched at precise points around the central thirty-one-foot cube of space at the entry. Color was applied to the back or bottom surfaces of these notches. Natural and artificial lights project this color back into the space around walls and fissures. The interior has a mysterious calm glow with surprising views as one moves around observing one field of reflected color through another and vice versa.

As the phenomena greatly reduces the intensity of the color being reflected, a range of fluorescent colors could be utilized on the unseen surfaces.

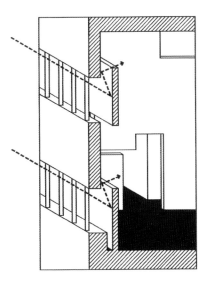

Facing page and right: Details of spatial
color reflection
Above: Diagram of daylit color projection

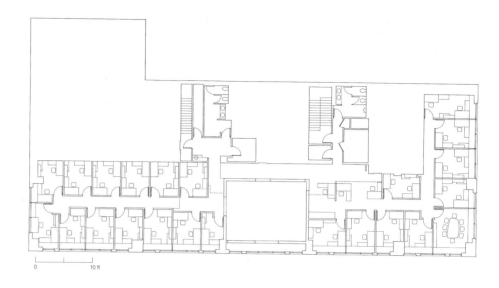

0   10 ft

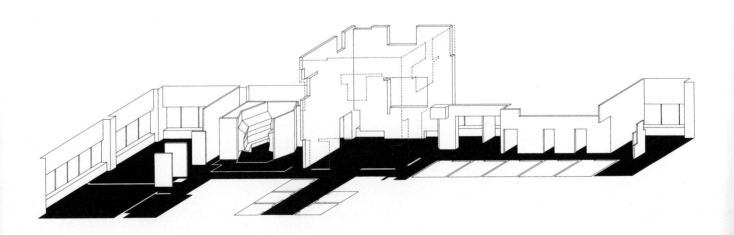

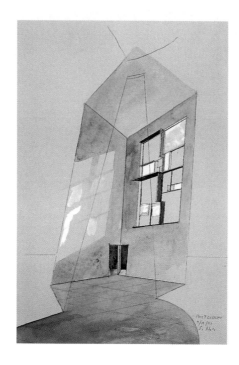

Chapel and Town Square
Port Ludlow, Washington, 1991

Port Ludlow is a new community on the site of a former saw mill on a small, deep-water bay in Washington. Different architects are at work on various parts of the town. The town square by Steven Holl and Don Carlson is a parallelogram with its acute angles oriented toward Admirality Bay to the north and toward the Cascade Mountains to the southwest.

One side of the town square is formed by four houses. The exteriors reinforce the collective space while the interiors are individually developed into a four-part ode to the Pacific Northwest. The first house is called A Walk Through the Forest, the second, Melancholia,

the third, Free Spirit, and the fourth, A Gaze at the Mountains.

The chapel, which might also serve as a meeting house, is programmed as a duality. As a meeting house it could accommodate gatherings such as receptions and concerts, but as a chapel, it becomes a place of silence and reflection, accommodating sacred events, such as small weddings, vigils, and memorial services.

The dual form of the building, curved and square, recalls the transformation of timber from the cylindrical trunks of the big douglas firs to their final milled form, rectangular in section. The round tower is inspired by the old saw mill burners, such as the one that existed in Port Ludlow. The curved interior space recalls the

mythical time of the ancient trees. The square section embodies the profane: ongoing historical time. The curved wall of the round tower is washed by sunlight from a tall south-facing window. The square tower is lit by the morning light from the east, which filters through a window of clear and cast colored glass, playing onto interior walls and the stained concrete floor.

A light wooden stair, passing inside the curved wall, leads to the upper roof. From the observation deck at the top, one can see the whole bay of Port Ludlow and beyond to the mountains. The steel structure, with scratch-coat stucco interior, is skinned in lead-coated copper that weathers to a silvery blue-gray.

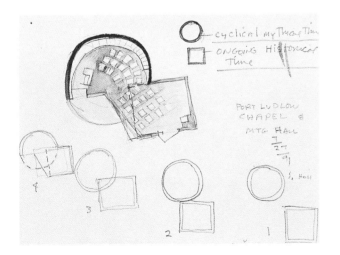

Above: Model of chapel and housing
Left: Concept sketch

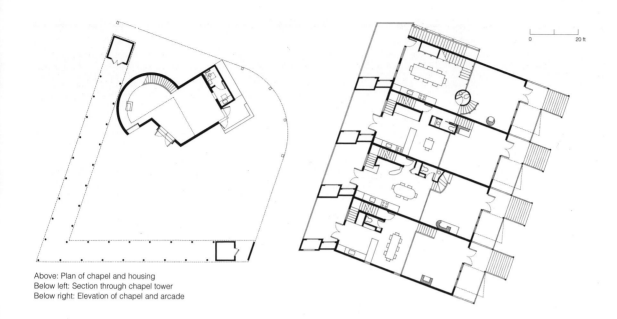

Above: Plan of chapel and housing
Below left: Section through chapel tower
Below right: Elevation of chapel and arcade

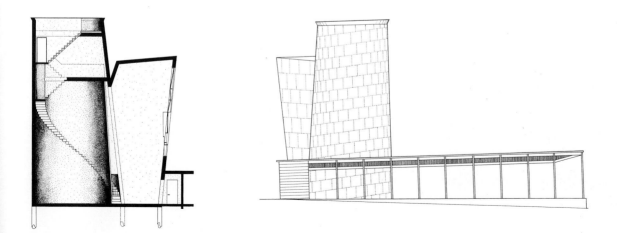

Architecture Building Addition
Andrews University
Berrien Springs, Michigan, 1992

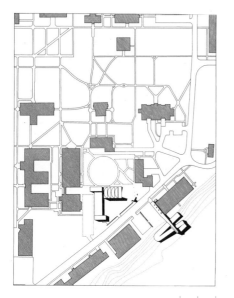

Above: Site plan
Below: Section

0   200 ft

The Andrews University campus in western Michigan is encircled on three sides by a sixty-foot-high bluff that separates the campus from lowland adjacent to the St. Joseph River. The Architecture Building Addition will be integrated into the campus to produce extended views that open and close between buildings, creating new spatial experiences along the students' various campus routes.

The Meander Studio begins on the plateau then goes over the edge into the gorge formed by the St. Joseph River; the Meander Studio drifts and rambles in a shifting horizon. Using lightweight technologically advanced materials, this building stretches the material into a space resisting standardization; it is subjective, not uniform. The studio thus negotiates between two horizons; the first is a positivist technological horizon whose goals of optimization and repetition are transcended in the second horizon of particularity, uniqueness, individuality, and subjective phenomenal understanding.

While the building's form is in a continuous transformation as it shifts horizons, the program is expressed in subtle changes. A rampway down connects the upper studio, the library, the jury rooms, and a new entry to the school. The library is housed in the first section of the building going over the edge of the ravine and is characterized by a continuously transforming roof that gradually shifts from concave to arched. As the building descends into the ravine, views out into the trees open along the bank; surrounding vegetation and wildlife become an extension of the interiors.

The continuous transformation of the section is expressed in a material transformation of the exterior aluminum skin. This skin changes to variations on corrugated aluminum as the building moves over the ravine. Other transformations of the aluminum, such as cast aluminum, characterize the architectural details. The structure is of point foundation steel pipe on approximately twenty-foot centers. This allows bays to be divided into three intermediates with metal decking spanning between. Floors are poured concrete with integral color. Interiors are natural light gray scratch coat plaster.

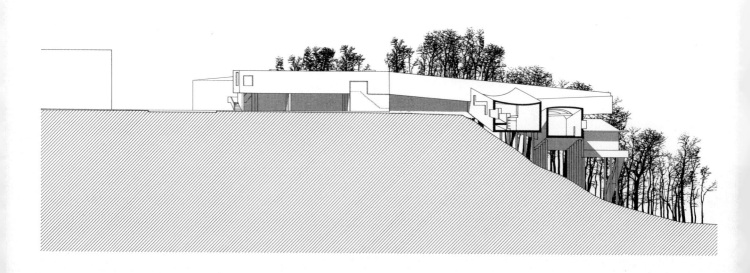

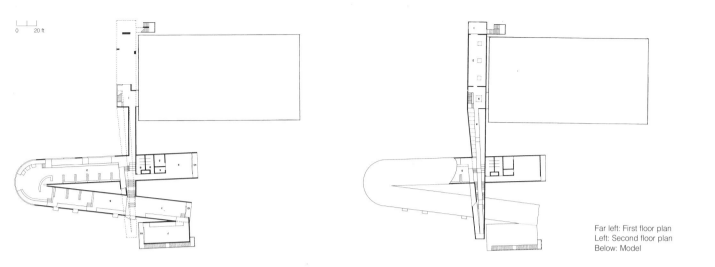

Far left: First floor plan
Left: Second floor plan
Below: Model

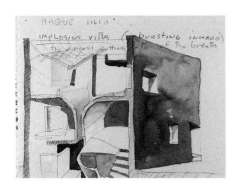

Implosion Villa
The Hague, Netherlands, 1992

Sited on the edge of a canal, the villa is part of a group of eight villas by eight different architects. Rather than emphasize the house as an object, courtyards and house are joined in an inward collapse.

Implosion Villa is an inversion of the modern courtyard house type, in which interior space is thrust outward and into the garden by large panes of glass and walls. In this villa, courtyard space implodes. Exterior spaces are pulled inward, making fissures into the body of the building. The fissures are warped counterclockwise into the body of the house beginning at the entrance court, where an indentation frees space for automobile doors.

The counterclockwise rotation of four courtyards and curvations pick up the clockwise rotation of the sun over and around the building, thus maximizing reflected light. The muted colors of the exterior stained brick are projected by the sun through the fissures into an interior of white plaster and white woodwork. Windows of bent glass chart the inward sucking of space in detail. Rubber floors and high gloss white ceilings draw in the outside light.

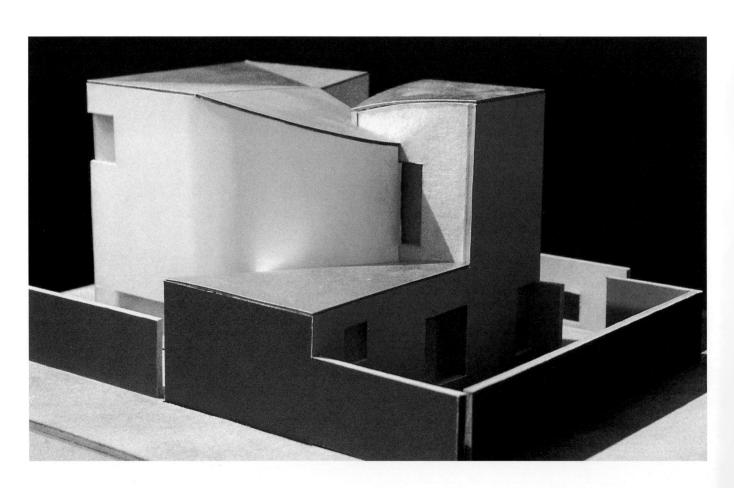

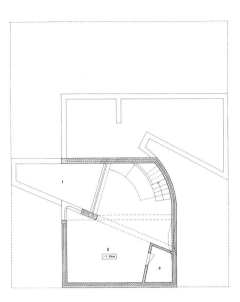

Lower level plan
1. Water Court
2. Studio
3. Utility

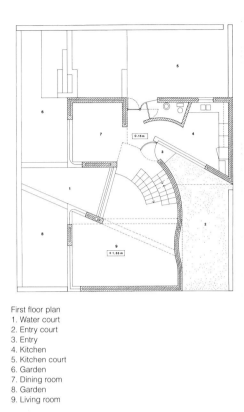

First floor plan
1. Water court
2. Entry court
3. Entry
4. Kitchen
5. Kitchen court
6. Garden
7. Dining room
8. Garden
9. Living room

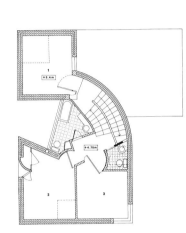

Second floor plan
1. Bedroom / Studio
2. Bedroom
3. Bedroom

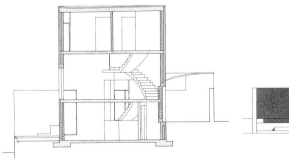

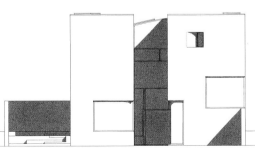

Far left: Section
Left: West elevation

Kiasma, Museum of Contemporary Art
Helsinki, Finland, 1998

The site for the museum lies in the heart of Helsinki. The Parliament Building is to the west, Eliel Saarinen's Helsinki Station to the east, and Alvar Aalto's Finlandia Hall to the north. The challenging nature of this site stems from the proximity of these monuments, the confluence of various city grids, and the triangular shape that potentially opens to Töölo Bay in the distance.

A *kiasma* occurs as the building's mass intertwines with the geometry of the city and landscape, which are reflected in the shape of the building. An implicit "cultural line" curves to link the building to Finlandia Hall while it also engages a "natural line" connecting to the east landscape and Töölo Bay. The landscape is planned to extend the bay up to the building in order to provide an area for future civic development along this tapering body of water, which also serves as a reflecting pool

for the Finlandia Hall and for the new development along its southern edge.

The horizontal light of northern latitudes is enhanced by a waterscape that serves as an urban mirror, thereby linking the new museum to Helsinki's Töölo heart, which on a clear day, in Aalto's words, "extends to Lapland." The changes in the building's elevation and the water extension and its shallow depth would allow for parking decks and/or highway linkages that are presently part of various planning considerations for the city. This water extension from Töölo Bay intertwines with and passes through the new museum. The rectangular pool along the west elevation of the museum is the source of a slow recirculating system that gradually lowers the water level. The gentle sound of moving water can be heard when walking through the cusp of the building section, which will remain open year round. These ponds are not intended to be drained. Instead, they freeze in winter according to a detail first devised by Eliel Saarinen for the accommodation of the

expansion of water during freezing. At night the west pond reflects the internal light radiating from the museum, expressing a spatiality of night. During the early evening hours of the winter months, glowing light escaping from the interior of the building along the west facade invites the public inside.

The Museum of Contemporary Art provides a variety of spatial experiences. We considered the range of contemporary artwork, and tried to anticipate the needs of a variety of artists, including those whose works depend on a quiet atmosphere to bring out their full intensity. An exhibition space that works for an expressive and unpredictable artist such as Vito Acconci must also work for artists such as Agnes Martin and Richard Tuttle. The general character of the rooms, which are almost rectangular with one wall curved, allows for a silent yet dramatic backdrop for the exhibition of contemporary art. These rooms are meant to be silent, but not static; they are differentiated through their irregularity.

The slight variation in room shape and size due to the gently curving section of the building allows natural light to enter in several different ways, which in turn drives movement through a series of spatial sequences. The overall design becomes a slightly warped gallery of rooms, where the spatial flow emerges from the combination of the horizontal-light-catching section and the continuity of the internal space. This curved unfolding sequence provides elements of both mystery and surprise that do not exist in a typical single- or double-loaded orthogonal arrangement of spaces. Instead, the visitor is confronted with a continuous unfolding of an infinite series of changing perspectives that connect the internal experience to the overall concept of intertwining or *kiasma*. There is a correspondence between the interior nearly rectangular spaces and the exterior continuous uninterrupted surface.

This open-ended spatial system suggests an expanse that lies beyond, in contrast to rectilinear organization and centered composition that dictate the viewer's movement and to an expressionist dynamic that excludes the serenity necessary for viewing some types of work. The spaces of the intertwining curves in *Kiasma* avoid both the rigidity of a classical approach and the excessive complexity of expressionism. The dynamic internal circulation, with its curving ramps and stairs, allows for an open, interactive viewing, inspiring visitors to choose their own routes through the galleries. Unlike a hierarchically sequenced or ordered movement, this open-ended, casual circulation provokes moments of pause, reflection, and discovery.

Another concept behind the building's spaces is to create silence by eliminating the intermediate scale in the building's architecture, thus making the walls neutral. In this way, the artwork can occupy the intermediate scale. Rather than articulating columns, moldings, and window openings, the architecture will be expressed through details such as the twist of a door handle, the edge of a stair, and the exposed thickness of a slab of glass.

A common problem in the design of an art museum with galleries on multiple levels is that the stacked section only permits natural light to enter the upper-level galleries, leaving the lower levels exclusively dependent on artificial light. In the Museum of Contemporary Art, we address this problem in two ways. First, horizontal light is deflected down through the section along the center. Second, the curved roof allows multiple skylights that refract light to galleries below the top level. Because of the building's curving and intertwining morphology, because of the interwoven torsion of space and light, the different levels are naturally lit.

Kiasma also serves as an art forum, open and flexible for staged events, dance and music performances, and seminars. Placing the cafe at ground level—open to both the garden and the lobby—makes it adaptable to informal events, such as poetry readings or round-table discussions. The auditorium, equipped with video capabilities, has a continuous glass rear elevation, making it visible from the outside passage through the building. When there is a lecture taking place in the theater, this open view might draw in observers who are walking along the passage to take part in the discussion.

With *Kiasma*, there is a hope to confirm that architecture, art, and culture are not separate disciplines but are all integral parts of the city and the landscape. Through care in development of details and materials, the museum provides a dynamic yet subtle spatial form, extending towards the city to the south and the landscape to the north. The geometry has an interior mystery and an exterior horizon that, like two hands clasping each other, form the architectonic equivalent of a public invitation. The interiors refer to the landscape and form the site that, in this special place and circumstance, is a synthesis of building and landscape . . . a *kiasma*.

A "line of culture" forms a link to Finlandia Hall, intertwining with a "line of nature" from the landscape and Töölo Bay

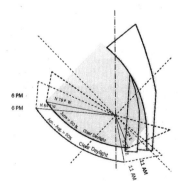

Utilizing the unique properties of natural light in a 60° north latitude, the primary curvature of the building forms a reversal of the sun path.

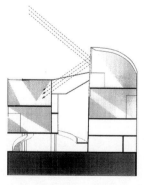

Light catching section: The curved section captures the warm light of horizontal sunlight.

Top: Photomontage of model in site.
Bottom: South elevation under construction,1997

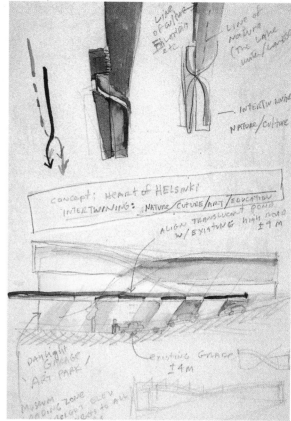

Left: Study models
Above: Concept sketch

Facing page
Top: Glitch drawing
Bottom left: Structural model
Bottom right: Competition computer model

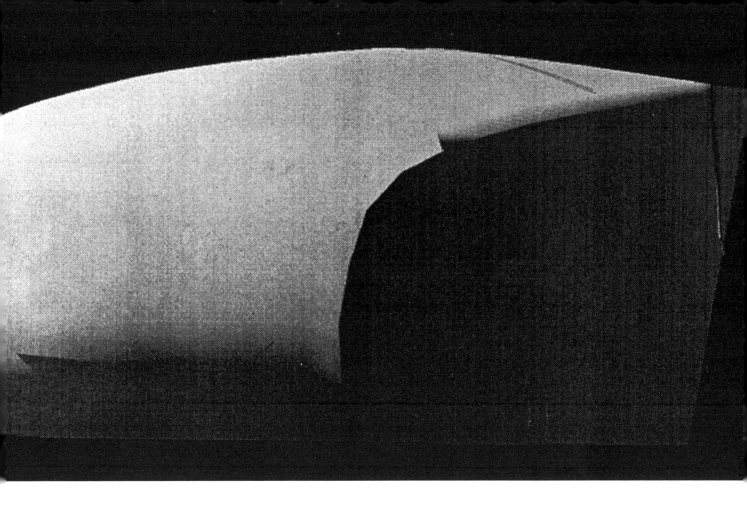

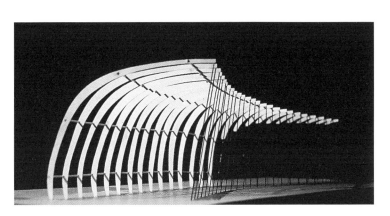

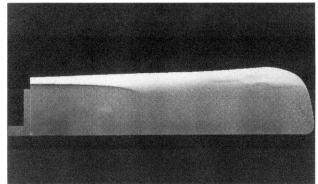

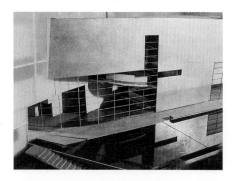

Model
Top: South elevation
Center: West elevation
Left: Detail of entry

Facing page top: View at night
Facing page bottom: Sections

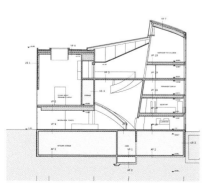

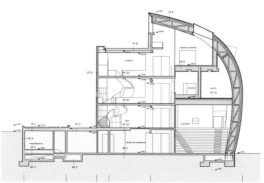

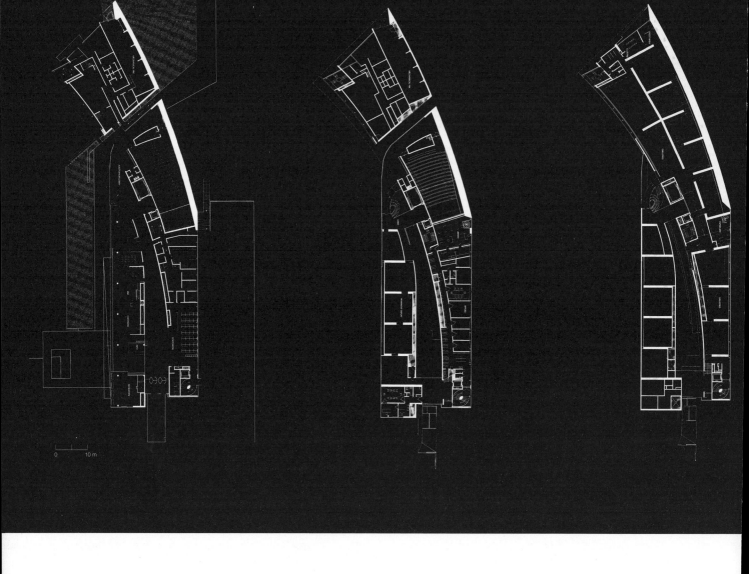

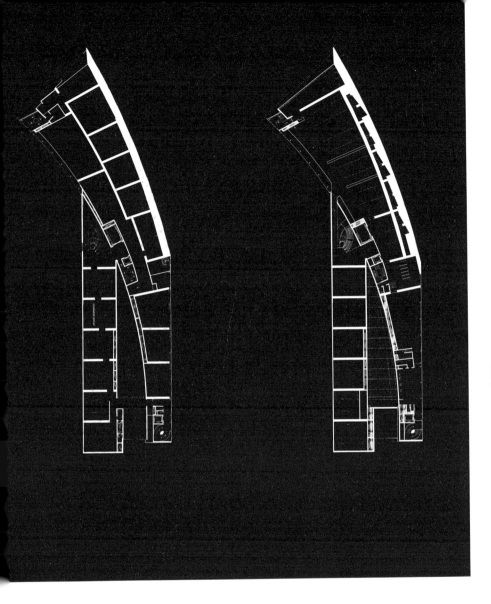

Left to right: First through fifth floor plans
Below: Construction view north from main entry lobby, 1997

Left: Interior view of skylight
Below: Gallery construction view, 1997

Below: Sections of bowtie skylight
Right: Half-scale mock up, exterior
bowtie skylight at night

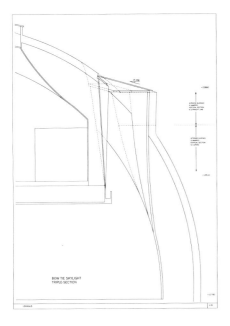

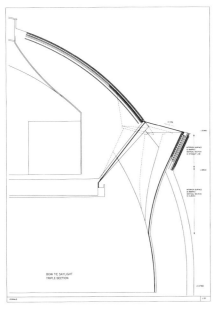

Left: Watercolor interior studies
Above: Interior view of half-scale mock-up
Facing page: Ground breaking 9 January 1996.
Artist Reijo Kela's performance work, like *kaskenpoltto*,
the ancient Finnish ground burning ritual in spring.

Urban Arms
Kaistrasse 18
Dusseldorf, Germany, 1993

Arms prepare the body for action. Added to an existing warehouse at Kaistrasse 18, these additions are in the form of five different areas or arms:

Floating Gallery Arm: Mounted on efficient flotation, falling and rising with the Rhine, this floating gallery has a glass roof. Strolling along the waterfront might be enlivened by looking down from the public promenade to the light of the gallery, even at night when the gallery is closed.

Bridge Gallery and Hanging Arm: The floating gallery access is enlivened by an optional second level access via a bridge gallery that also defines the main entry.

Rhine-View Arm: From this part of the vertical tower are magnificent views of the Rhine from each level. Spaces are organized as double height lofts; second or third levels can be added by tenants.

Solarium Arm: This obscure glass portion of the tower allows for maximum sunlight and a glowing effect at night.

Horizon Arm: From these two-level studios, the horizon is in full view from each garden terrace.

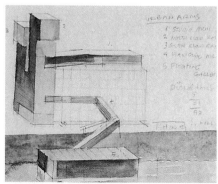

Concept sketch

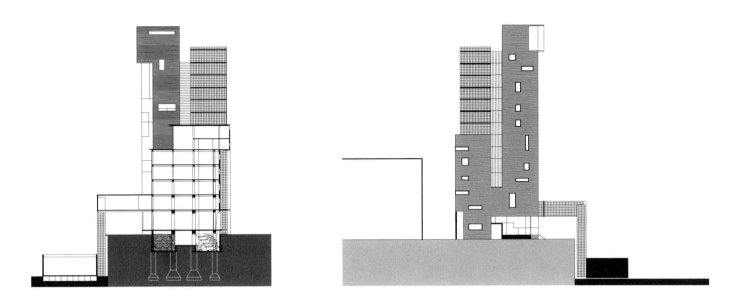

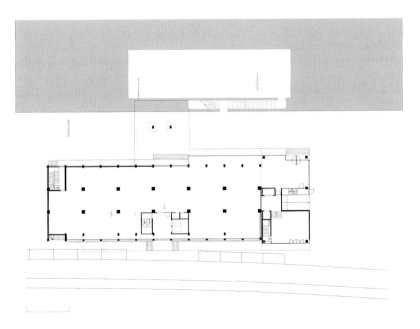

Facing page: Model at night
Above left: West section
Above right: East elevation
Left: Plan

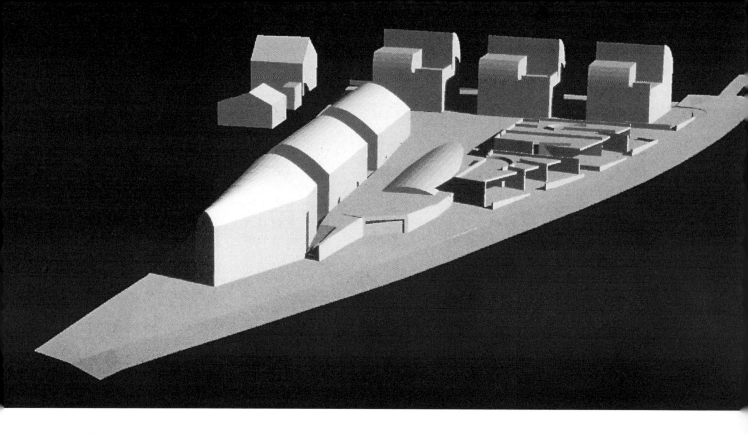

Zollikerberg Housing
Zollikerberg, Switzerland, 1993

A group of Spartan innovative apartments form
a semi-public garden enclosure on a hillside
near Zurich. In contrast to the suburban
sprawling apartment buildings nearby (with
no consideration for spaces in between), this
housing shapes and gives character to
exterior spaces. Individuation of the houses
provides a character of place and a quality of
orientation.

These houses, like human personalities, are
planned in differing psychological types. On the
east are the Apollonian types—three white
villas, thirteen meters cubed, into which a circle
is drawn in section organizing the curving roof.
Each Apollonian villa contains five apartments
of varying sizes. Interiors are characterized by
rotating walls giving hinged-space flexibility for
various interior layouts. Construction is cavity
wall with white plaster. To the south are the
Dionysian types. These are garden villas with
grape arbors and meandering garden walls. To
allow south sun into the main public garden,
these houses are only one and one-half levels
high. They help form a landscape viewed from
the other villas. Construction is in concrete

block and insulated translucent glass. To the
north are the Daedalus types. Silently watching
over the Dionysians and the Apollonians, these
houses are formed in the shape of a wooden
cow, separated into three sections. Each section contains one-level apartments on the lower
floors and duplex apartments on the upper
floors. Construction is concrete frame with
Eternit siding.

An underground parking area with pre-cast
curved roof is naturally ventilated and lit by the
stair openings to the east and the west. This
curved-roof space may also be used for
community gatherings or events.

Facing page: Computer model
This page top: Concept sketch
This page bottom: Views of model

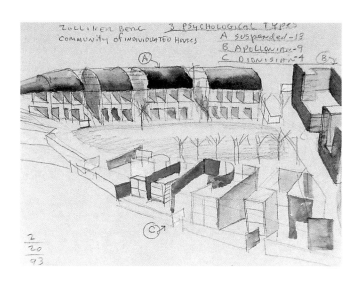

Top: Third floor plan
Bottom: Ground floor plan

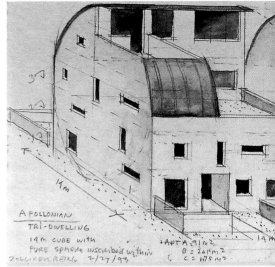

A POLLONIAN
TRI-DWELLING

14 m CUBE WITH
PURE SPHERE INSCRIBED WITHIN
ZOLLIKENBERG 7/27/93

APT A = 91 m2
B = 26 m2
C = 1475 m2

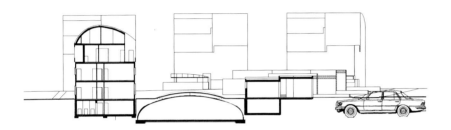

Top: Elevation of Apollonian villas
Center: Section through Dionysian and
Daedalus types
Bottom: Section through garage,
elevation of Daedalus types

StoreFront for Art and Architecture
New York, New York, 1992–93

Steven Holl and artist Vito Acconci were commissioned to renovate the aging facade of the StoreFront for Art and Architecture. The project is the second collaborative effort by Holl and Acconci; their first work together was a 1988 urban plan for a growing arts community in downtown Washington D.C. sponsored by the Pennsylvania Avenue Development Corporation.

StoreFront for Art and Architecture is situated on the corner of a block that marks the intersection of three distinct neighborhoods: Chinatown, Little Italy, and SoHo. The gallery itself is a limited, narrow wedge with a triangulated exhibition interior, such that the most dominant structure for StoreFront is the building's long facade. In fact, the history of exhibitions at the gallery was marked in the various cuts and layers of paint that exhibiting artists and architects had imposed on and through this once-uniform surface.

Drawing from this history, neither Acconci nor Holl were interested in the permanence of the facade or the idea of a static gallery space. Seeking to introduce improbability and to puncture the facade, Acconci and Holl challenged this symbolic border that underlines the exclusivity of the art world, where only those on the inside belong. Using a hybrid material comprised of concrete mixed with recycled fibers, Holl and Acconci inserted a series of hinged panels arranged in a puzzle-like configuration. When the panels are locked in their open position, the facade dissolves and the interior space of the gallery expands out onto the sidewalk.

If the function of a facade is to create a division separating the inside from the outside space, this new facade, in the words of StoreFront director Kyong Park, is "No wall, no barrier, no inside, no outside, no space, no building, no place, no institution, no art, no architecture, no Acconci, no Holl, no StoreFront."

Below: Site plan
Facing page top: Open hinged panels
Facing page bottom: Plan

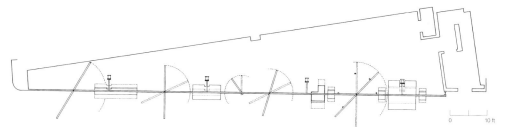

Above: Detail of facade incision
Right: Closed and open facade
Facing page: Facade at night

Above: Steven Holl and Vito Acconci with model
Right and facing page: Views of interior

Makuhari Housing
Chiba, Japan, 1992–1996

The new town of Makuhari is sited on dredged fill at the rim of Tokyo Bay. The urban planners have set rules for building-height limits, tree-lined streets, and areas for shops. Each city block is to be designed by three or four different architects in an effort to achieve variety.

Our concept interrelates two distinct types: silent, heavyweight buildings and active, lightweight structures.

Lightweight = Activists = Sounds
Heavyweight = Bracketing Blocks = Silence

The silent buildings shape the forms of urban space and passage. The concrete bearing-wall structures have thick facades and a rhythmic repetition of openings (with variation in window or deck). Apartments are entered via the inner garden courts. Slightly inflected according to the path of the sun, they gently bend space and passage, interrelating with movement and the lightweight structures.

A celebration of miniature and natural phenomena is taken up in the lightweight activist force of individual characters and programs. These individuated "sounds" invade the heavyweight "silence" of the bracketing buildings.

Inspired by Bashō Matsuo's *The Narrow Road to the Deep North*, the semi-public inner gardens and the perspectival arrangement of activist houses form an inner journey.

The interiors of apartments in the silent buildings are designed by Koichi Sone and Toshio Enomoto (Kajima Design). The activist structures by Steven Holl include: East Gate House, Sunlight Reflecting House; North Gate House, Color Reflecting House; North Court House, Water Reflecting House; South Court House, House of Blue Shadow (Public Meeting Room); West Gate House, House of Fallen Persimmon; South Gate House, House of Nothing (Public Observation Deck).

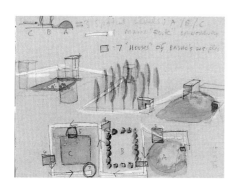

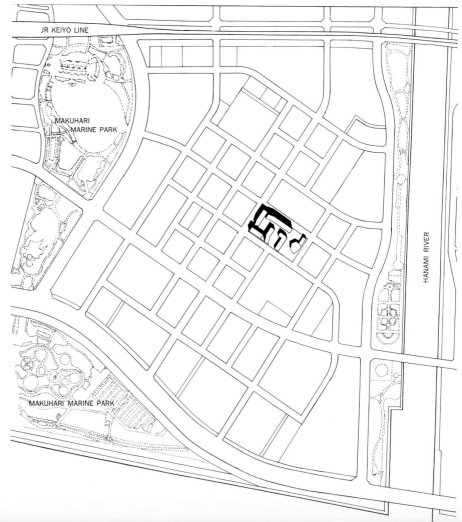

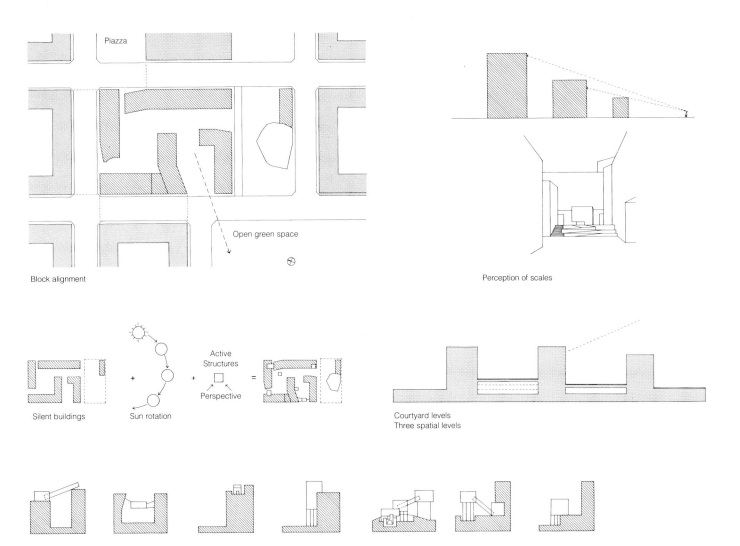

Piazza

Open green space

Block alignment

Perception of scales

Active
Structures

+

Perspective

=

Silent buildings   Sun rotation

Courtyard levels
Three spatial levels

Correlational chart
Urban relation: figure / ground

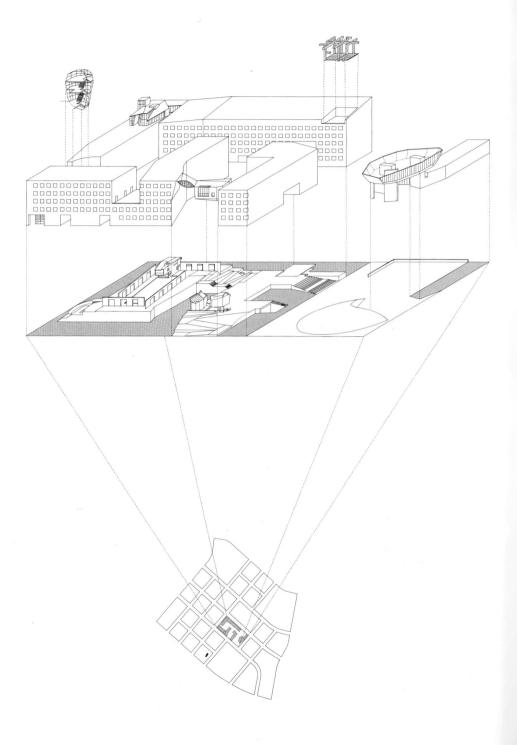

Early axonometric of activist / silent buildings

Model view from south

View from the northwest, 1996

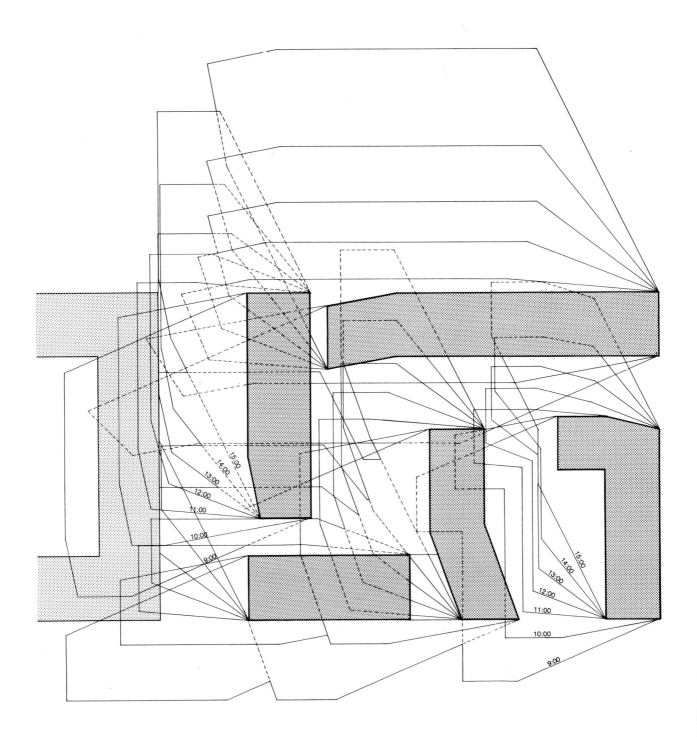

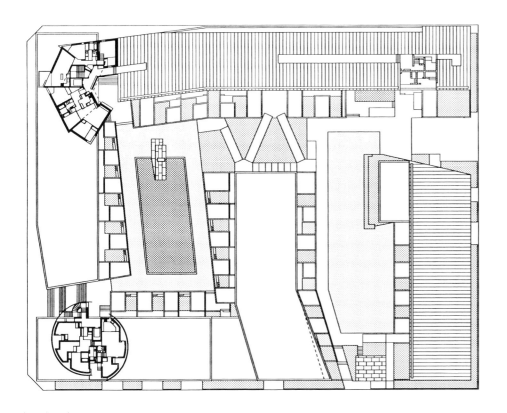

Facing page: Sun calculation
By Japanese code each apartment
must have four hours of sunlight
per day
Left: Roof plan
Below: Section looking northeast.
The buildings rest on over 600 piles
driven 20 meters into the landfill
of Tokyo Bay. The parking garage is
a combination of three layers:
mechanical systems, parking, and
natural ventilation

0   10 m

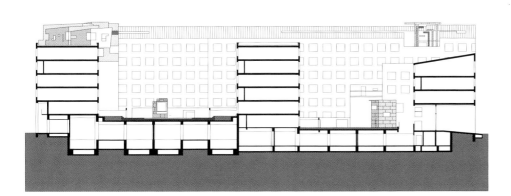

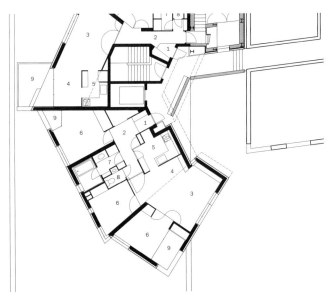

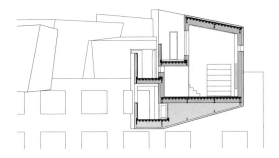

East Gate House
(Sunlight Reflecting House)
1. Entrance
2. Aisle
3. Living room
4. Dining room
5. Kitchen
6. Bedroom
7. Washroom
8. WC
9. Balcony

0   5 m

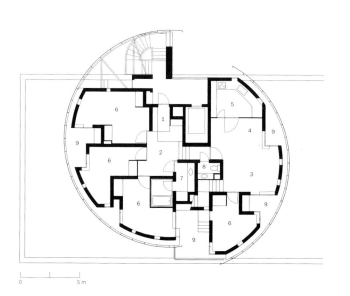

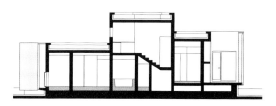

North Gate House
(Color Reflecting House)
1. Entrance
2. Aisle
3. Living room
4. Dining room
5. Kitchen
6. Bedroom
7. Washroom
8. WC
9. Balcony

0   5 m

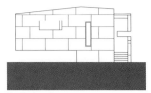
South elevation

East elevation

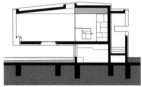
Section

West elevation

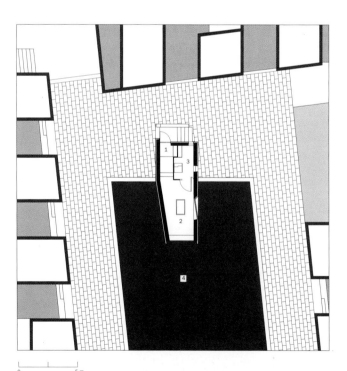

North Court House
(Water Reflecting House)
1. Entrance
2. Tea Room
3. Kitchen
4. Reflecting Pool

0   5 m

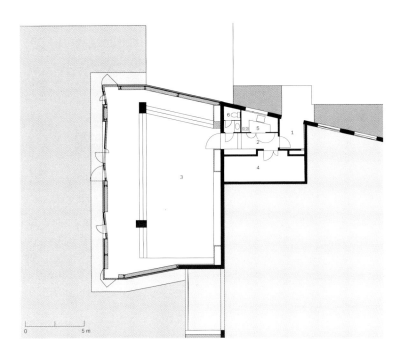

South Court House
(House of Blue Shadow)
1. Entrance
2. Aisle
3. Meeting room
4. Storage
5. Kitchen
6. WC

Below: View through passageway
toward South Court House

0   5 m

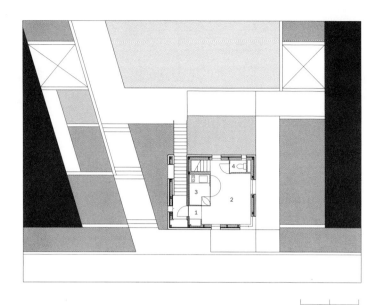

View toward West Gate House

West Gate House
(Fallen Persimmon House)
1. Entrance
2. Living / Dining Room
3. Kitchen
4. WC
5. Bedroom
6. Washroom
7. Balcony

0   5 m

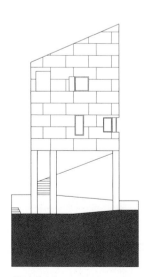

West elevation

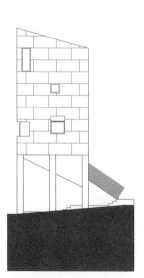

South elevation

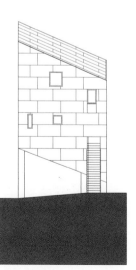

East elevation

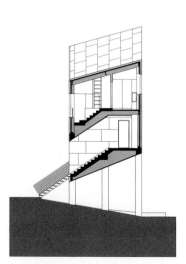

Section

South Gate House (House of Nothing)

Floor plan

0   5 m

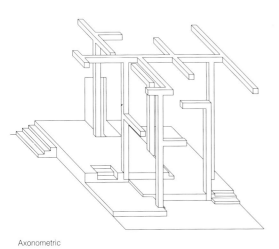

Axonometric

Views from south
Top: Early watercolor perspective
Bottom: Construction January 1996

View of North Court from east
Top: Early watercolor perspective
Bottom: Construction January 1996

Hypo-Bank Offices and Art Hall
Munich, Germany, 1994

The site is the better portion of a city block fronting on Theatinerstrasse in the heart of the old city center of Munich. The project is a hybrid of many functions: offices, a banking hall, shopping facilities, apartments, an art hall, and related facilities such as parking. The plans of the lower voids are extruded upwards, forming a glass-peaks level of glazed apartments.

As a counter-offering against the banal qualities of the tourist-oriented "shopping-mall" transformation of old European city centers, our project organizes urban life in three overlaps of function and time and in the following priority: time one, permanent community of in-city residents; time two, semi-transient office workers and urban commuters; time three, transient tourists and passing shoppers.

To organize the maximum quality and range of living spaces and experiences for the described time layers, a heuristic device was adapted: a musical score by Karl Stockhausen for a piece entitled *Gruppen* (inspired by a view of the Alps). The score shows a mountain range in the first three measures and shaped voids in the remaining four measures.

Top: Site collage
Above: *Gruppen*, K. Stockhausen, 1955
Facing page
Top left: Concept sketch
Bottom left: Sculpture garden on roof
Bottom right : Site plan

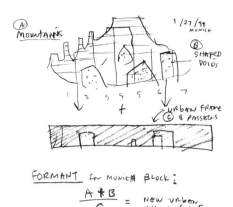

FORMANT for MUNICH BLOCK:

$$\frac{A * B}{C} = \text{NEW URBAN WAYS OF LIFE}$$

Stockhausen's 7 TUTTI

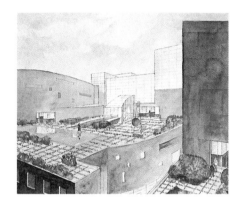

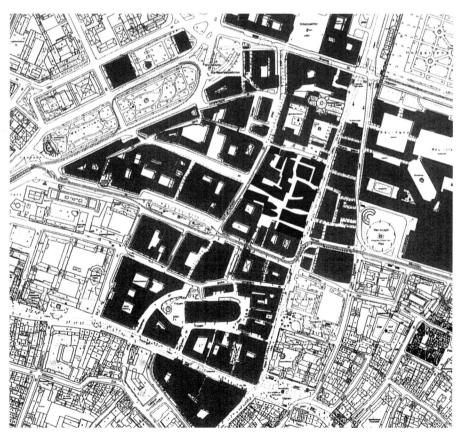

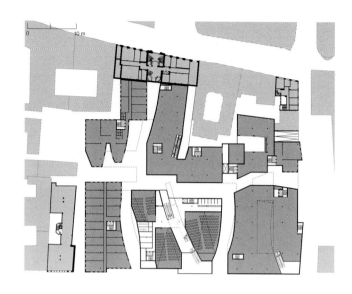

Level 1 plan

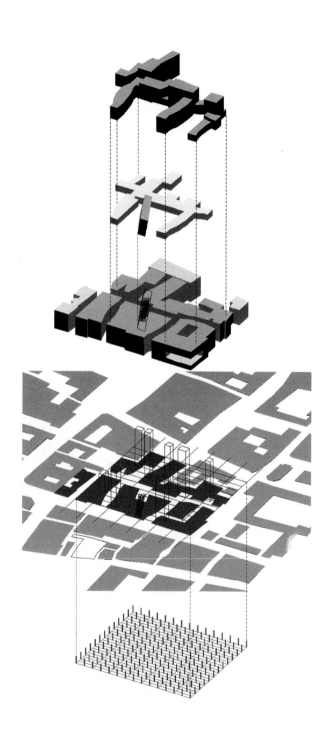

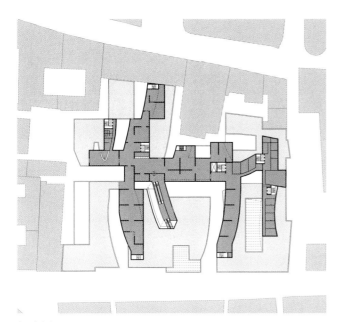

Level 4 plan

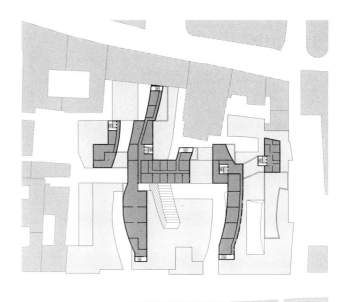

Art Hall plan

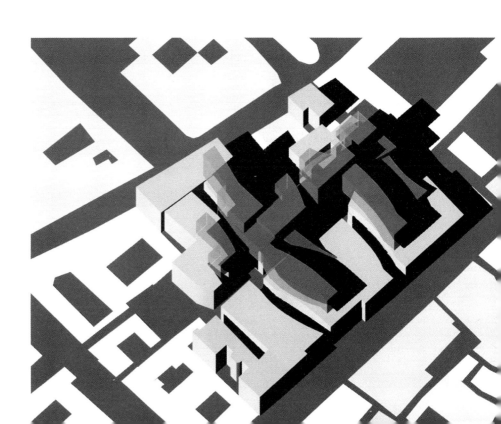

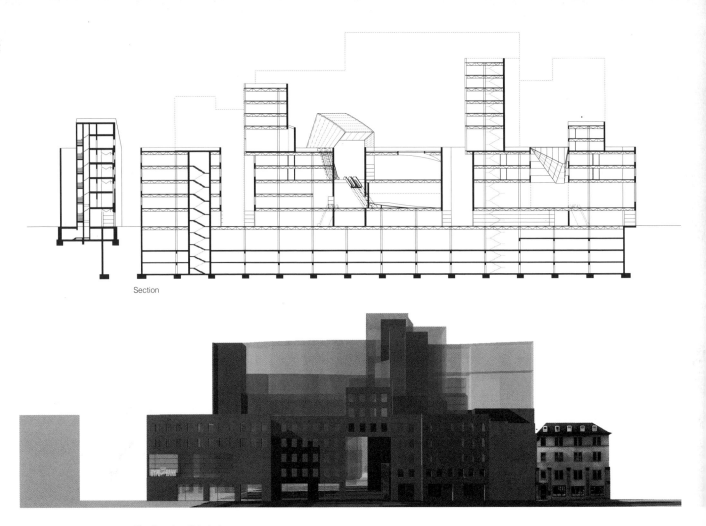

Section

Elevation along Salvatostrasse

Above: The urban block has sponge-like qualities; its extruded inner hollows are pushed upward into glass apartments.
Right: Escalators to upper public levels

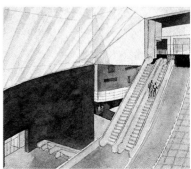

Manifold Hybrid
Amsterdam, Netherlands, 1994—

In mathematics, "the way to get a geometrical manifold is to take a polyhedral chunk from a geometrical space and identify its faces pair-wise with each other."
—George Francis, *A Topological Picture Book*

Situated on the reused shipping quays over-looking the Erts Canal, this large housing block of 182 apartments is part of an urban plan for housing that calls for three superblocks in a lower urban field of garden row houses. The eighteen-story block with several functions (offices, a small art gallery, a restaurant, a boat house, a deli, and a health club) is envisioned as a section of a new city. Eleven different apartment types are accessed by very different paths.

The rotations and translations of this fifty-six-meter cube, manifold building are seen from below as colored folds. The heart of the block is a huge water court that can accommodate visiting houseboats in the Amsterdam tradition. The penetrating stain on the concrete is of black, blue, and yellow colors that guide visitors on the multiple routes within.

The view to Amsterdam's horizon is an important asset to these apartments, while the inter-locking geometry of the sections adds a unique dimension to the interiors. Just as the interior is a harbor of the soul, the *U*-shaped building is itself a harbor with a section of a small city surrounding it on three sides.

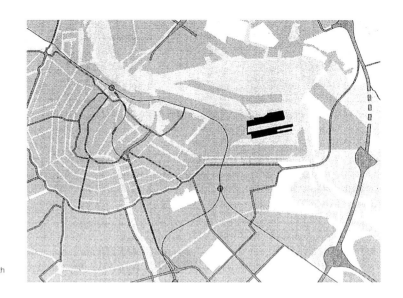

Central Amsterdam with
Borneo Sporenburg

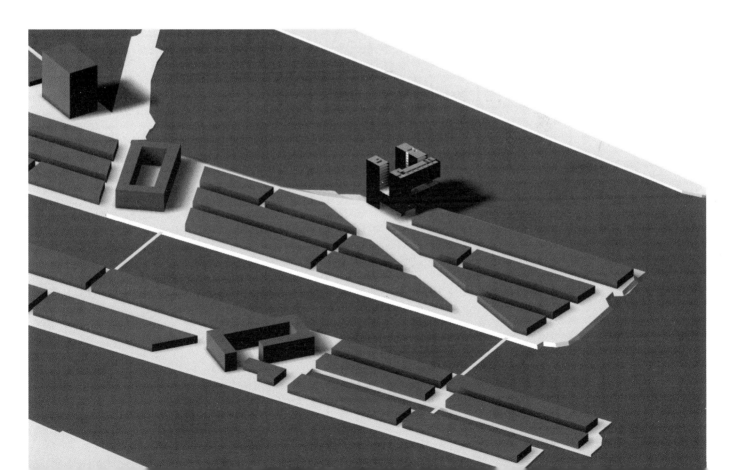

The most ambitious of the hybrid programs,
a rappel wall climbing course, will be installed
on the north facade with three–four levels
of difficulty

The canal enters the building, allowing for direct
ferry links to the Amsterdam central station

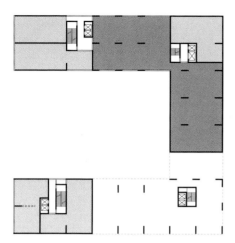

Third floor plan
Luxury apartments and offices

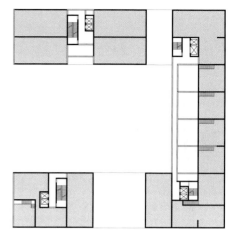

Sixteenth floor plan
Small apartments and luxury apartments mixed

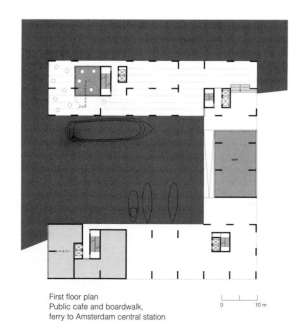

First floor plan
Public cafe and boardwalk,
ferry to Amsterdam central station

0   10 m

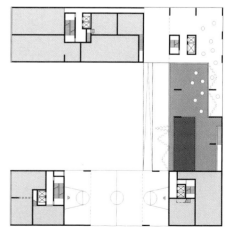

Eighth floor plan
Restaurant and gymnasium

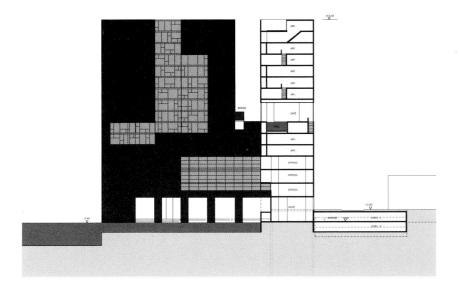

Research has shown that recognizing a human at ground level from a high-rise window reaches a limit at the seventh floor. At the seventh level here we insert an open space with public activities.

I Project Residence
Seoul, Korea, 1995–

I Project is an interwoven garden and building complex for the chairman of a large corporation. The complex program of the residential, office, family, recreational, and banquet functions are expressed in the *weave* of parts. Like the close intertwining of the corporation and family life embodied in the program, the weave expresses an interdependent relationship. "Mansion" is dissolved into individual dwelling areas.

The weave concept aims at a woven open flux of habitation, trees, and plantings. It is as distinct from the object-building as are the two urban fields of Seoul: Kangnam with its isolated towers and Kangbuk with its more finely scaled, ecological pattern. The concept allows

for a natural expression of bringing light to the lower levels through the natural gaps in the weave.

Various spaces within the weave are equipped for testing new ecological techniques and equipment. For example, some gardens are test sites for hydroponics growing technology. A special earth of glass wool is fed nutrients by tiny tubes regulated by computer. (There are large-scale implications for such gardens in regards to the diminishing of the earth's topsoil.) A state-of-the-art photovoltaic cell weave is balanced with a ground-water heat exchanger to develop a complete climate-controlled environment without the use of fossil fuels.

Roofs are of Rheinzink weathered to a soft green-grey to blend with the garden landscape. Screens are of several woven types; some in

stainless steel with shading screens built in to afford maximum sun control. Other screens are in reddened weathered brass, glass and cable, and sand-blasted glass. The overall effect is a weave of shimmering transparencies and semi-transparencies that enhance the mysterious glow of the natural light.

In the increasing fragmentation of our times, the weave concept reaches for intangibles—spiritual life, connection with nature, the interrelatedness of all peoples on our planet.

The basic principles of *feng shui* guide the arrangement of the weave to insure a positive flow of all energies. The main dining room is positioned and shaped to align with a magnificent view of the mountain of the vermilion bird, connecting to the geomantic spirit of ancient Seoul.

Urban diagram, Seoul

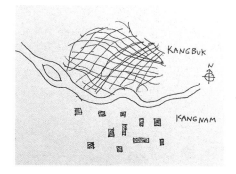

Weave concept diagram, I Project

Four guardian directions of Seoul

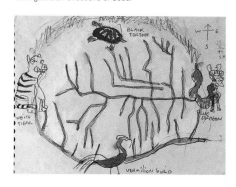

Neighborhood context

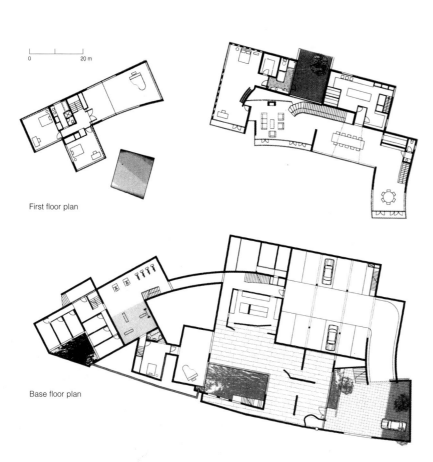

First floor plan

Base floor plan

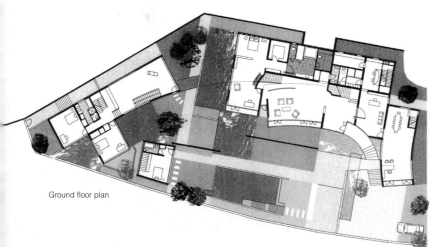

Ground floor plan

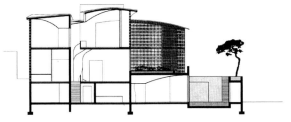

Section through main building

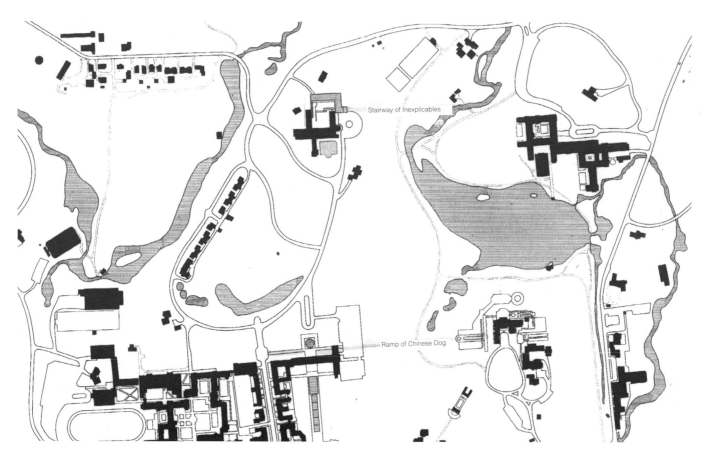

Stairway of Inexplicables

Ramp of Chinese Dog

Cranbrook Institute of Science
Bloomfield Hills, Michigan, 1991–

This addition to the Cranbrook Institute of Science continues the bracketing and shaping of exterior spaces with buildings that characterize the Cranbrook campus. Our aim is to make the least intrusion on the architecture of Eliel Saarinen's Institute of Science (1931–33) while maximizing the potential for future circulation.

The new inner garden has a gently sloping and folding connection to the exterior campus grade. At the northwest corner the addition does not touch the ground, allowing space to flow in and out. This "permeable" connection gives the garden exhibits orientation and flexibility and makes the space open and inviting.

A new axis from the new entry, called "Stairway of Inexplicables" is roughly parallel to the existing Ramp of the Chinese Dog. This new line of view and movement connects the institute to existing nature trails along the sloping ground to the east.

The original Saarinen building, presently divided into the Hall of Minerals and Hall of Man, is physically invigorated by an addition that opens the dead-end circulation of these galleries. The slipped "U" shape, like the scientific diagram for strange attractors, allows for multiple paths within the exhibitions and other programs of the Institute. The term "strange attractors" (coined by the meteorologist Edward Lorenz) has geometric and experiential potential. From Lorenz's *Exploring Chaos*:

Whichever direction you have come from, you still have a choice. Moreover, points that start close together get stretched apart as they circulate round the attractor, so they "lose contact," and can follow independent trajectories. This makes the sequence of lefts and rights unpredictable in the long term. This combination of factors stretching points apart and "re-injecting" them back into small regions is typical of all strange attractors.

With this concept as an analog, we aim for an open-ended addition that can easily adapt to change. Its various circuits have unique qualities that allow for the potential that no visit to the new science museum will be a repeat experience, rather each engagement is provocative and unpredictable. It is as much about the flow of energy as about architectural form.

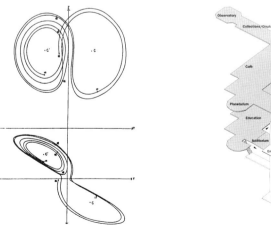

Facing page: Plan of Cranbrook campus with
expansion of the Institute of Science
Above: Site model
Far left: Lorenz's diagram of strange attractors
Left: Program diagram

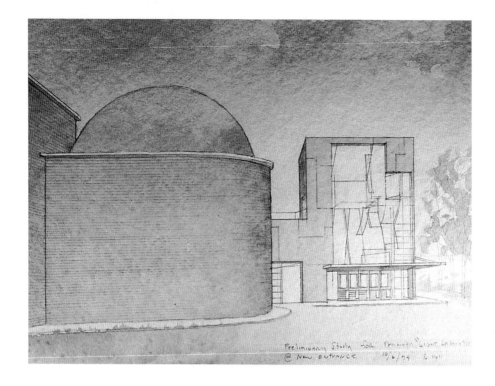

Preliminary Study for Prismatic Light Laboratory @ New Entrance 10/6/04 S. Holl

On axis with the visitor's approach, the new Entry Hall is designed as a "light laboratory." The wall is composed of seven types of glass, each exhibiting different phenomena by casting light onto the plaster walls and ceiling. Prismatic panels project spectrums, cast and sandblasted glass diffuse and absorb light, bent and angled glass demonstrate reflection, and slumped/laminated lenses refract light into varying patterns.

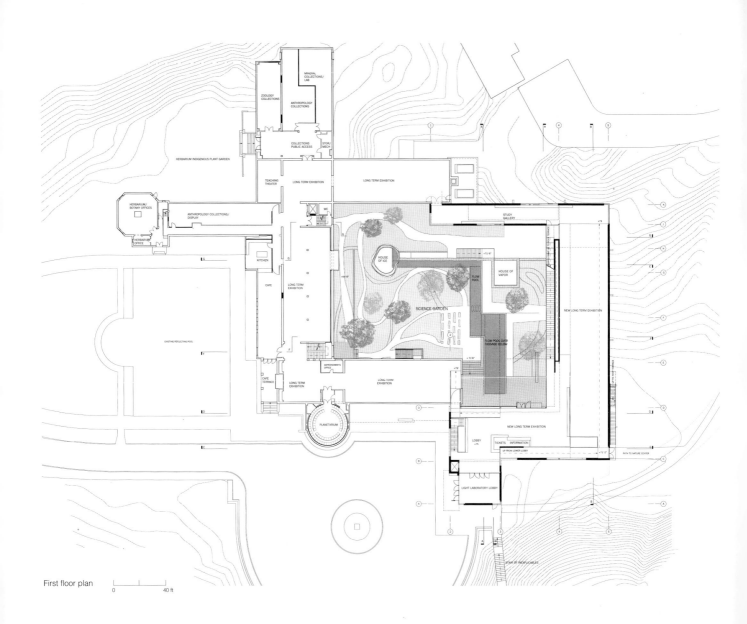

First floor plan

0   40 ft

South elevation

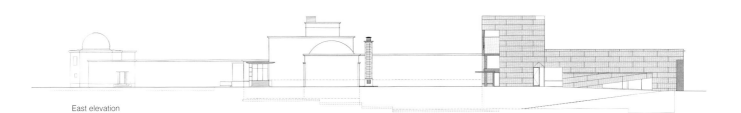

East elevation

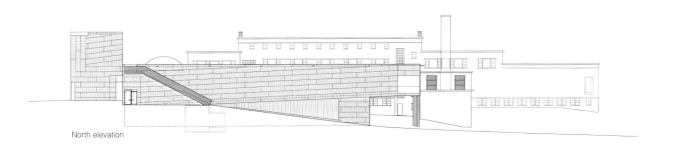

North elevation

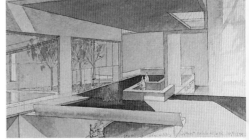

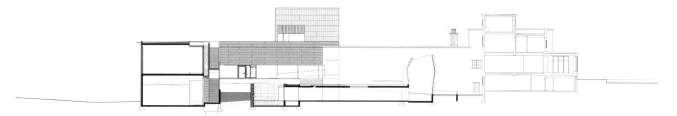

Section EE through Science Garden looking east

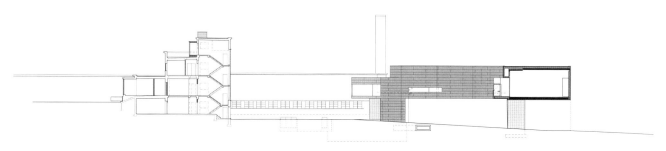

Section GG through Science Garden looking west

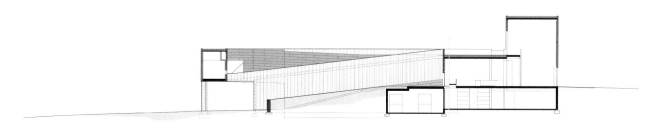

Section HH through Science Garden looking north

The Science Garden exhibits are continued in a passage below the Flow Pool.
One exhibit (below left) demonstrates the
mechanical and phenomenal properties
of a roller weir.

In the new Science Garden natural and scientific phenomena are exhibited in the open air. The focus of the Science Garden, "The Story of Water," is an exhibit of three states of water embodied in three features: the Flow Pool, the House of Vapor, and the House of Ice. Along with the plantings of the garden, these features illustrate the intense seasonal changes of the area. Multiple paths within the garden lead to areas for group gathering and teaching, as well as to private benches located within the planting. From large trees to individual flowers, the planting is arranged to highlight the color cycles and fragrances of the four distinct changing seasons.

The House of Vapor (top right) is a chamber in which water is atomized into a continuously changing fine mist. It can be experienced from both the exhibit passage below and the garden above. The fine mist creates a micro-climate for special planting. Warm high-quality exhaust air from the new building propels the mist upward and allows the exhibit to function year round.

The House of Ice (facing page, bottom right, at end of Flow Pool) exhibits the incredible forms and properties of ice. It is an open-topped, wire mesh structure on which ice forms and remain frozen for five months of the year. Its location in the southwest corner of the garden takes advantage of the existing building walls to keep it shaded during much of the winter. From the exhibit passage below, visitors can enter its conical structure and view the sky through walls of ice.

Chapel of St. Ignatius
Seattle University
Seattle, Washington, 1994–1997

He returns to his metaphor of light: the light to perceive what can best be decided upon must come down from the first and supreme wisdom.—David Lonsdale, S.J., *Eyes to See, Ears to Hear*

The metaphor of light is shaped in different volumes emerging from the roof whose irregularities aim at different qualities of light. The concept, a gathering of different lights, can be seen in the concept sketch of bottles of light emerging from a stone box. Just as no single method is prescribed in the Jesuits' spiritual exercises, here a unity of differences is gathered into one.

Each of the light volumes corresponds to a part of the program of Catholic worship. The south-facing light corresponds to the procession, a fundamental part of the mass. The city-facing north light corresponds to the Chapel of the Blessed Sacrament and to the mission of outreach to the community. The main worship space has a volume of east and west light.

At night, which is the time when masses take place in this university chapel, the light volumes are like beacons shining in all directions out across the campus. On many occasions, these lights shine throughout the night. In the narthex and entry procession, one experiences the natural light of the sun with its play of shadows. Moving deeper into the chapel the light has a mysterious glow of reflected color fields; the

complimentary color of each field is set within a stained glass lens.

The different lights are: procession, natural sunlight; narthex, natural sunlight diffused; nave, yellow field with blue lens (east) and blue field with yellow lens (west); Chapel of the Blessed Sacrament, orange field with purple lens; choir, green field with red lens; Reconciliation Chapel, purple field with orange lens; bell tower and pond, projecting and reflecting night light.

The chapel is sited to form a new campus quadrangle to the north, the west, and, in the future, to the east. The elongated rectangular plan is especially suited to defining campus space as well as the processional and gathering space within. Directly to the south of the chapel is a reflecting pond or "thinking field."

Left: Concept sketch, "Bottles of Light"
Facing page: Mixture of color of reflected light and complementary color of glass lens.

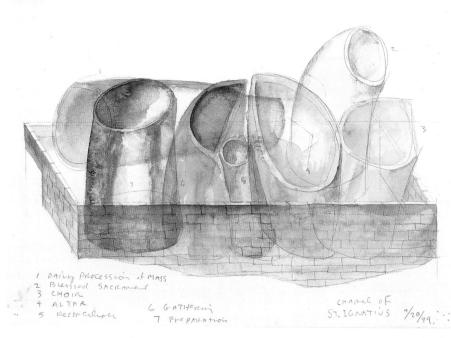

7 Different "Bottles of Light" in a stone box

1 Daily Procession of Mass
2 Blessed Sacrament
3 Choir
4 Altar
5 Reconciliation
6 Gathering
7 Preparation

Chapel of St. Ignatius 9/28/99

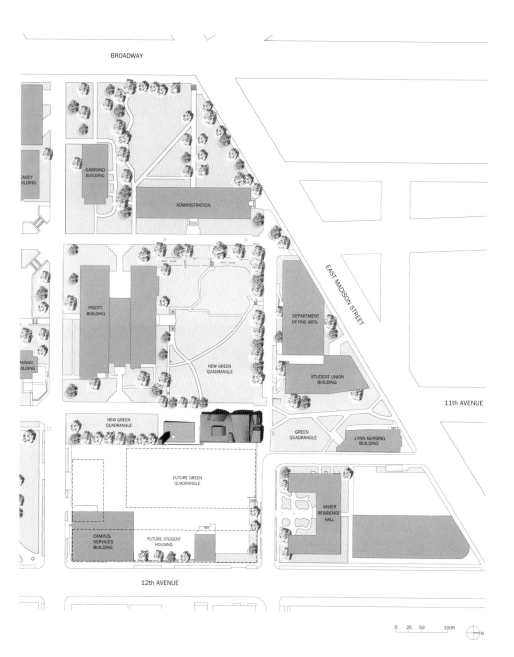

BROADWAY

CASEY
BUILDING

GARRAND
BUILDING

ADMINISTRATION

PIGOTT
BUILDING

NANNAN
BUILDING

NEW GREEN
QUADRANGLE

EAST MADISON STREET

DEPARTMENT
OF FINE ARTS

STUDENT UNION
BUILDING

11th AVENUE

NEW GREEN
QUADRANGLE

GREEN
QUADRANGLE

LYNN NURSING
BUILDING

FUTURE GREEN
QUADRANGLE

KAVIER
RESIDENCE
HALL

CAMPUS
SERVICES
BUILDING

FUTURE STUDENT
HOUSING

12th AVENUE

0 25 50   100ft

N

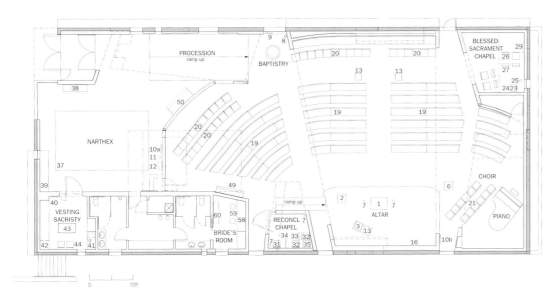

Liturgical furniture legend

1. Altar	11. Candle for book	25. Tabernacle lamp	39. Bench
2. Ambo	12. Stand for book	26. Chairs for meditation	40. Clock
3. Presider's chair	13. Ancillary tables	27. Prie-dieu	41. Sacrarium
4. Deacon / Minister chair	14. Vessels for mass	28. Candle offering	42. Censer cabinet
5. Acolyte Seating	15. Vessels for holy oils	31. Confessor's chair	43. Vesting table
6. Cantor's stand	16. Fixed cross (above)	32. Penitent's chair	44. Chairs
7. Candle stand	19. Pews	33. Penitent's prieu-dieu	49. Marian shrine
8. Pascal candle stand	20. Movable chairs	34. Movable privacy screen	50. Patron shrine
9. Ambry for holy oils	21. Choir chairs	35. Table / book stand	58. Vanity table
10. Processional cross	23. Tabernacle	37. Carpet	59. Vanity stool
	24. Tabernacle stand	38. Brochure rack	60. Bench

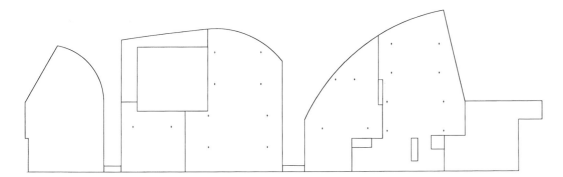

Left: West elevation showing pick pockets of tilt-up construction
Below: Tilt-up construction

Exterior light at night

Top: Worm's-eye view of early study model
Bottom: Interior view, 1997

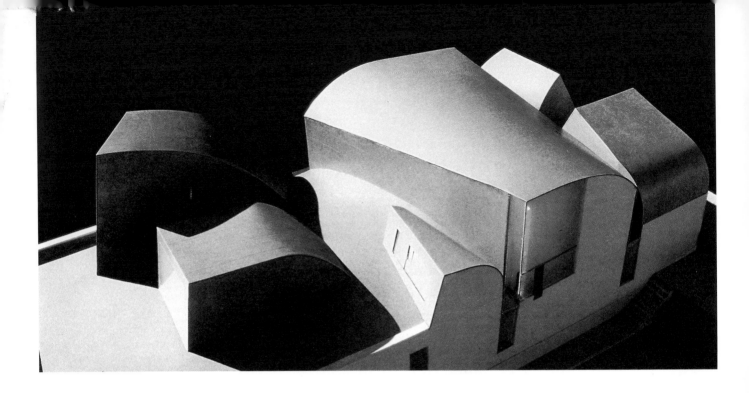

Above: Roof of model
Right: Roof of chapel, 1997

This page
Above: Ceiling, model study of reflected / projected light
Left: Light baffle in Reconciliation Chapel

Facing page
Top: Light baffle in choir
Bottom: View towards entry

LIST OF SELECTED WORKS

DATE	PROJECT	COLLABORATORS/ASSISTANTS
1989–91	**Void Space / Hinged Space Housing**	Hideaki Ariizumi* Pier Copat
1989–91	**Stretto House**	Adam Yarinsky* Kent Hikida Stephen Cassell Terry Surjan
1990	**Palazzo del Cinema**	Janet Cross† Peter Lynch Stephen Cassell Jun Kim Adam Yarinsky
1989	**Stitch Plan**	Peter Lynch Patricia Bostch Pier Copat Ben Frombgen Bryan Bell
1989	**Spatial Retaining Bars**	Peter Lynch Pier Copet Ben Frombgen Janet Cross
1988	**Erie Canal Edge**	Pier Copat Ben Frombgen Bryan Bell
1990	**Spiroid Sectors**	Janet Cross† Tod Fouser Peter Lynch Scott Enge Hal Goldstein Chris Otterbein Laura Briggs
1990	**Parallax Towers**	Peter Lynch Romain Ruther
1991	**D. E. Shaw & Company Offices**	Thomas Jenkinson* Janet Cross

DATE	PROJECT	COLLABORATORS/ASSISTANTS
1991	**Chapel and Town Square, Port Ludlow**	Janet Cross Scott Enge Todd Fouser Adam Yarinsky Thomas Jenkinson
1992	**Architecture Building Addition**	Thomas Jenkinson* Adam Yarinsky* Tomoaki Tanaka Stephen Cassell Mario Gooden Terry Surjan Annette Goderbauer
1992	**Implosion Villa**	Tomoaki Tanaka Mario Gooden Janet Cross Terry Surjan
1998	**Kiasma, Museum of Contemporary Art**	Janet Cross† Vesa Honkonen* Justin Rüssli Chris McVoy Tomoaki Tanaka Pablo Castro-Estévez Justin Korhammer Tim Bade Anderson Lee Anna Müller Tapani Talo Jan Kinsbergen Lisina Fingerhuth Terry Surjan Kwang Paik Competition team: Janet Cross† Mario Gooden Stephen Cassell Thomas Jenkinson Tomoaki Tanaka Justin Rüssli Molly Blieden

LIST OF SELECTED WORKS

DATE	PROJECT	COLLABORATORS/ASSISTANTS	DATE	PROJECT	COLLABORATORS/ASSISTANTS
1998	**Kiasma (continued)**	*Juhani Pallasmaa Architects:*	1994–	**Manifold Hybrid**	Justin Korhammer*
		Timo Kiukkola*			Justin Rüssli
		Timo Ruusuvuori			Anderson Lee
		Seppo Sivula			Lisina Fingerhuth
		Seppo Mäntylä			
		Heikki Määttanen	1995	**I Project**	Justin Rüssli*
					Justin Korhammer
1993	**Urban Arms**	Justin Rüssli*			Tomoaki Tanaka
		Jan Kinsbergen			Jan Kinsbergen
		Gundo Sohn			Stephanie Forsyth
					Bradford Kelley
1993	**Zollikerberg Housing**	Justin Rüssli*			Heleen Van Heel
		Stephen Cassell			
		Justin Korhammer	1991–	**Cranbrook Institute of Science**	Janet Cross†
		Tim Bade			Chris McVoy*
		Lisina Fingerhuth			Pablo Castro-Estévez
					Anna Müller
1992–93	**StoreFront for Art and Architecture**	Vito Acconci†			Jan Kinsbergen
		Face Fabrications			Terry Surjan
					Adam Yarinsky
1992–96	**Makuhari Housing**	Tomoaki Tanaka*			Stephen Cassell
		Anderson Lee			Annette Goderbauer
		Sumito Takashina			Bradford Kelley
		Sebastian Schulze			
		Mario Gooden	1997	**Chapel of St. Ignatius**	Tim Bade*
		Gundo Sohn			Jan Kinsbergen
		Bradford Kelley			Justin Korhammer
		Lisina Fingerhuth			Janet Cross
		Anna Müller			*Olson Sundberg Architects:*
		Justin Korhammer			Rick Sundberg†
		Jan Kinsbergen			Tom Kundig*
		Thomas Jenkinson			Jim Graham
		Janet Cross			Janice Webb
		Terry Surjan			
		Hideaki Ariizumi**	*Project Architect		
		Kajima Design†	**Consultant		
		Koichi Sone & Assoc.†	†Collaborator		
1994	**Hypo-Bank Offices and Mixed-Use Retail**	Justin Rüssli			
		Justin Korhammer			
		Marie-Therese Harnoncourt			
		Anderson Lee			
		Tim Bade			
		Tomoaki Tanaka			

PUBLISHED WRITINGS BY STEVEN HOLL

Pamphlet Architecture 1-10, Princeton Architectural Press, New York, 1998.

"Twofold Meaning." *Kenchiku Bunka* (July 1998).

Jussi Tiainen, photographer. *Kiasma*. Helsinki: Museum of Contemporary Art, 1998.

Kiasma: Working Process (catalog for the exhibition). New York: Architectural League, 1995.

"Pre-Theoretical Ground." *Columbia Documents of Architecture and Theory*. 1995, 27–57.

"Kain Tapper: The Artist and His Work." *Kain Tapper: Tombs in Wood* (exhibition catalogue). New York: Stuart Levy Fine Art Gallery, 1994, 7.

"Raw Experience." *Architectures of Herzog and DeMeuron*. New York: Peter Blum Editions, 1994, 25–26.

"Questions of Perception: Phenomenology of Architecture." *A+U Special Issue* (July 1994), co-authors Alberto Pérez Gómez and Juhani Pallasmaa.

"Steven Holl: Intertwining Verweben." *Color of an Architect*. Hamburg: Galerie fur Architektur, June 1994.

"Steven Holl." *Bau-Kunst-Bau*. Milan: *Domus*, 1994, 132–45.

GA Architect 11—Steven Holl (January 1993; collected works.

"Phenomenon and Idea." *Columbia University Newsline, Graduate School of Architecture, planning and Preservation* (March/April 1993): 2.

"Representing Building." *Lotus International* (1993): 116–131.

"Steven Holl: Edge of A City." *Urban Forms, Suburban Dreams*. Malcolm Quantrill and Bruce Webb, eds. College Station: Texas A&M University Press, 1993, 121–128, cover.

Steven Holl. Bordeaux and Zurich: Artemis & Arc en Reve Centre d'Architecture, 1993.

"Locus Souless." *The End of Architecture? A Documentation of Vienna Conference 15 June 1992*. Munich: Prestel-Verlag, 1993: 35–46.

Pamphlet Architecture 13: Edge of a City, New York: Princeton Architectural Press, 1991.

"Edge of a City exhibition at the Walker Arts Center." *Columbia University Newsline,*

Graduate School of Architecture, planning and Preservation (March/April 1991): 4.

Anchoring, Third Edition. New York: Princeton Architectural Press, 1991.

Wrede, Stuart, ed. *Emilio Ambasz/Steven Holl: Architecture*. New York: Museum of Modern Art, February 1989; exhibition catalogue, 14–23.

"Within The City: Phenomena of Relations." *Design Quarterly* 139 (Spring 1988): 1–30.

"Typological Variations on a Rail Structure: Bridge of Houses in Manhattan." *Lotus International* (1984): 41–45.

"Foundations, American House Types." *Precis* 4. New York: Columbia University, 1983, 36–37.

Pamphlet Architecture 9: Urban and Rural House Types. New York: Pamphlet Architecture, Ltd., 1982.

"Anatomy of a Skyscraper." *Cities—The Forces That Shape Them*. Edited by Liza Taylor. New York: Cooper-Hewitt Museum, 1982, 68–69.

"Conversation with Alberto Sartoris," *Archetype* (Fall 1982).

Pamphlet Architecture 7: Bridge of Houses. New York: Pamphlet Architecture, Ltd., 1981.

Pamphlet Architecture 5: The Alphabetical City. New York: Pamphlet Architecture, Ltd., 1980.

"USSR in the USA" *Skyline* (1979).

"The Desert De Retz." *100% Rag: Student Quarterly, Syracuse School of Architecture* (1978): 5–6.

"Review of the Blue Mountain Conference." *Skyline* (1978).

Pamphlet Architecture 1: Bridges. New York: Pamphlet Architecture, Ltd., 1977.

BIBLIOGRAPHY
1998

Agassi, Joseph. "A Question of Perception: Between Architect & Philosopher." *Architecture of Israel* (vol.34): 4-15; Kiasma, Makuhari.

Bell, Micahel. "Over Dilation, Over Soul." *Slow Space* (1998):384-407; Kiasma.

Giovannini, Joseph. "Architecture in Motion." *House Beautiful* (September 1998): 70-73; Kiasma.

Lecuyer, Annette. "Iconic Kiasma." *The Architectural Review* (August 1998): 46-53; Kiasma.

Schjeldahl, Peter. "Brave Old World." *Village Voice* (July 7, 1998); Kiasma.

"Steven Holl: Kiasma." *Quaderns* (September 1998)

Stein, Karen. "Breaking the Mold, Kiasma Museum, Helsinki." *Architectural Record* (August 1998): 86-99.

"Steven Holl: Kiasma, Museum of Contemporary Art, Helsinki." *Architecture and Urbanism* (August 1998): 16-37.

Temin, Christine. "Captivating Museum Puts Helsinki on Art World Map." *Boston Globe* (July 26, 1998).

Kudalis, Eric. "Holl's Redone Design Gets Go-Ahead for Minnesota Architecture School." *Architectural Record* (July 1998): 33.

Amstutz, Brian. "Steven Holl/Kiasma, Museum of Contemporary Art." *Kenchiku Bunka* (July 1998): 22-57.

"Kiasma, Museum of Contemporary Art." *Space*, (July 1998): 78-87.

Lord, Roberta. "Holl's Kiasma Comes to Light." *Architecture* (June 1998): 27.

Webb, Michael. "Steven Holl's Newest Luminous Masterwork." *Metropolis* (May 1998): 74-79; Kiasma, Chapel of St. Ignatius.

"Steven Holl: Residence and Y Retreat." *GA Houses 55* (1998): 68-75.

Fang, Eric. "From Brown Field to Biotech Campus in San Francisco." *Competitions* (Spring 1998): 54-67; UCSF Mission Bay competition.

Remmele, Mathias. "Kiasma, Museum fur zeitgenossische Kunst in Helsinki." *Bauwelt* (March 1998): 476-484.

Kennedy, Ken. "Form, Space, Light." *Monument #17* (February 1998: 64-81; Selected Projects.

"Kiasma." *Project Magazine (N*o. 78, 1998).

"Kiasma." *Projekti Uutiset*, No. 1 (1998): 4-33.

"Kirchenbau: Es werde Licht." *Hauser* (1998).

Ingersoll, Richard. "Holl's Northern Lights." *Architecture* (January 1998): 76-81; Kiasma.

"Kiasma." *Form Function Finland* No.69 (January 1998).

Drewes, Frank. "Room of Light." *Light & Architecture* (January 1998): 18-23; Chapel of St. Ignatius.

Birnbaum, David. "Almost Finnished." *Artforum*

(January 1998): 41; Kiasma.

"Steven Holl." *Imagining the Future of The Museum of Modern Art.* Abrams, New York, 1998:170-179; MoMA Competition.

1997

Rouch, Larry. *Arcade, The Journal for Architecture and Design in the Northwest*, (Winter 1997):30; Bellevue Art Museum.

"MoMA and Magma, 10 Projects for the Museum of Modern Art." *Lotus* (December 1997); MoMA Competition.

"Makuhari Housing in Tokyo." *DBZ* (November 1997); Makuhari.

"Profile: Steven Holl." *Architectural Profile* (October 1997): 39-86.

Safran, Yehuda. "The Chapel of St. Ignatius at Seattle University." *Domus*, No. 796 (September 1997): 18-27.

Faith & Form, Journal on Religion, Art & Architecture, vol XXX, No. 2 (1997): cover; Chapel of St. Ignatius

"Congregation of Light." *Architectural Review* (August 1997): 25-33; Chapel of St. Ignatius

Olson, Sheri. "Steven Holl's Glowing Chapel in Seattle." *Architectural Record* (July 1997): 40-53.

"The Making of St. Ignatius." *Arcade* (Summer 1997).

"Makuhari 2001 in der Bay of Tokyo." *Bauwelt*, 9 (May 1997).

"Cranbrook Institute of Science." *Casabella* (April 1997): 28-35.

Stein, Karen. "Steven Holl's Triumph in Japan." *Architectural Record* (January 1997): 64-77.

"Honor Awards: Knut Hamsun Center, Norway and Museo Cassino, Italy." *Architecture* (January 1997): 72-3, 88-9.

Ibelings, Hans. "Americanism: Dutch Architecture and the Transatlantic Model." (1997): 91; Manifold Hybrid

"Design on the Cutting Edge." *Competitions* (Summer 1997): 26-27;University of Texas-Houston Medical Center.

1996

Cramer, Ned. "On the Boards." *Architecture* (January 1996): 43.

"Steven Holl."*Architectural Profile.* (September 1996):82-9.

"Museum of Contemporary Art, Helsinki Finland." *Hinge* (1996): 36-38.

Zaera-Polo, Alejandro. "A Conversation with Steven Holl."*Arcade* (Fall 1996): cover, 14, 15; Chapel of St. Ignatius.

"Housing Block in Makuhari, Japan."*Domus* (June 1996):10-19.

Nobre, Ana Luiza. "Steven Holl Arquitectura para sentidos."*AU* (June/July 1996): 79-85;Kiasma, Fukuoka)

"Makuhai Bay-Town Patios 11."*Shinkenchiku* (1996):131-141.

Futagawa, Yukio. "Makuhari Housing."*GA Architect* (May1996): 8-167

1995

Riley, Terence. *Light Construction* (catalog for the exhibition). New York: Museum of Modern Art, 1995, 68-71; 138-143.

Frampton, Kenneth. "Stretto House." *American Masterworks: The Twentieth Century House.* New York: Rizzoli, 1995, 291-99.

Ojeda, Oscar Riera, ed. "Stretto House." *The New American House: Innovation in Residential Design and Construction.* New York: Watson-Guptil in association with Whitney Library of Design, 1995, 96–101.

Ryan, Raymund. "Isolated Luminosity." *The Architectural Review* (November 1995): 54–55; Chapel of St. Ignatius.

Merkel, Jayne. "Steven Holl at the Architectural League." *Oculus* (November 1995): 5; *Kiasma*, Museum of Contemporary Art.

Dixon, John. "The Intertwining." *Progressive Architecture* (October 1995): 74–83; *Kiasma*, Museum of Contemporary Art.

"Projektion." *AIT: Architektur Innenarchitektur Technischer Ausbau* (October 1995): cover, 76–79; D. E.Shaw.

Knauf, Brigitte. "Licht=Farbe=Licht." *Ambiente* (September–October 1995): 74–77; D. E. Shaw.

Stein, Karen. "Architecture." *New York* (11 September 1995): 62; Light Construction exhibition review.

Widder, Lynette. "Educating Our Perception." *Diadalos* (August 1995): 64–73; selected projects.

Muschamp, Herbert. "When the Museum Itself is the Artwork." *New York Times,*

18 August 1995; Architectural League *Kiasma* exhibition review.

Newhouse, Victoria. "Architecture: Museums as Art, New Spaces for the Next Century." *Architectural Digest* (July 1995): 40; *Kiasma*, Museum of Contemporary Art.

"New York Apartment Design." *Space Design* (September 1995): 138–43; Metropolitan Tower Apartment.

Sciarreta, S. "Interview with Steven Holl." *Op. Cit.* (January 1995): 5–15.

"Gathering and Reflecting Light." *Progressive Architecture* (June 1995): 54; Chapel of St. Ignatius.

"Steven Holl: *Kiasma*, Museum of Contemporary Art." *GA Document* 43 / *GA International* '95 (May 1995): 40–45.

Sullivan, Ann C. "On the Boards." *Architecture* (May 1995): 43; Cranbrook Institute of Science.

Aveioglu, Gökhan, Özlem Ercil, and Ayhan Ozan. "Profil: Steven Holl." *Arredamento* (May 1995): 66–80; selected projects.

Betsky, Aaron. "De Architectuur van Steven Holl." *de Architect* (April 1995): 28–49; selected projects.

Dijk, Hans van. "Recent Projects: An Interview with Steven Holl." *Archis* (April 1995): 36–47; selected projects.

"Steven Holl: Makuhari Housing, Zollikerberg Housing." *GA Houses* 45 (April 1995): 76–82.

Vukic, Fedja. "Steven Holl." *VIDI* (Spring 1995):54–56.

Kirkpatrick, Ron. "Steven Holl: Perception and Material." *Ark, Journal Department of Architecture at University of Florida* (Spring 1995): 8–9.

Goldberger, Paul. "Houses as Art." *New York Times Magazine*, 12 March 1995: 54–55; Stretto House.

"Steven Holl." *Architectural Design* (January–February 1995): 40–45; Stretto House.

1994

Vercelloni, Matteo. "Steven Holl: New York Storefront." *Abitare* (November 1994): 190–93.

Esche, Jan. "Steven Holl: Galerie fur Architektur, Hamburg, Germany." *Die Bauwelt* (July

1994); exhibition review.

Neumeyer, Fritz, Paolo Belloni, and Paola Iacucci. "La Strana Coppia." *Construire* (August 1994): 106–07; StoreFront for Art and Architecture.

Drewes, Frank F. "Storefront, N.Y.C." *Deutsche Bauzeitschrift* (August 1994): 12.

Calatroni, Sergio. "Sensitive Space: Architecture in Light." *Luce Annual* (1994): 25; D. E. Shaw.

"Wohnüberbauung in Fukuoka, Japan 1991." *Werk, Bauen & Wohen* (6 June 1994): 28–30.

"D. E. Shaw & Co. in New York, U.S.A." *Architektur & Wettbewerbe* (June 1994): 44–45.

Bekaert, Geert. "Storefront." *Archis* (June 1994): 50–51.

MacKeith, Peter. "One Year Later: Still a Hotly Debated Subject." *Competitions* (Summer 1994): 44–51; *Kiasma*, Museum of Contemporary Art.

Watanabe, Hiroshi. "Western Architects in Japan." *Design Quarterly* (Summer 1994); Fukuoka.

"Competition for the Museum of Contemporary Art, Helsinki." *Compe & Contest* (May 1994): 25–28.

"Architecture and Water. Steven Holl: Stretto House and Chiasma." *Architectural Design* (1994): 40–45.

"Steven Holl." *Taiteen Maailma* (April 1994): 24–28.

Rochon, Lisa. "Inside Out" *INSITE* (May 1994): 43–45; StoreFront for Art and Architecture.

"A Clean Sweep." *New York Times Magazine,* 10 April 1994: 20–23; Stretto House.

MacNair, Andrew. "Urban Arms: The Arm of Architecture." *Architecture &Urbanism* (April 1994): 28–38; Urban Arms.

Connah, Roger. "Letter from the Suburbs of the Suburbs." *Any* (March/April 1994): 60–62, *Kiasma*.

"The Periphery." *Architectural Design Profile* (March/April 1994): 86–89; Edge of a City.

Faiferri, M. "Fenomenologia Architettonica: Una Mostra su Steven Holl." *L'Industria delle Costruzioni* (March 1994): 46–47.

Blank, Ylva. "Holl to Hell Tycker Norri." *Arkitektur* (March 1994): 56–57; *Kiasma*.

Sartoris, Alberto. "Steven Holl." *Archithese*

(March/April 1994): 10–60; selected works.

Leclerc, David. "Steven Holl." *L'Architecture d'aujourd'hui* (February 1994): cover, 86–109; six projects.

Norri, Marja-Riita. "Musee a Helsinki: Explications et Controverse." *Architecture d'aujourd'hui* (February 1994): 110–115.

Stephens, Suzanne. "All in the Name of Architecture." *Oculus* (January 1994): 5; Storefront for Art and Architecture.

Slatin, Peter. "Holl and Acconci Reface Storefront." *Architecture* (January 1994): 23.

Thurell, Soren. "Interview: Steven Holl." *Arkitektur* (January 1994): 36–41; *Kiasma*.

1993

"Steven Holl: Concours du Musee d'Art Contemporain d'Helsinki." *Architecture d'Aujourd'hui* (December 1993): 46–47.

"Steven Holl: Espace Pense, Espace Percu." *Techniques et Architecture* (October/November 1993): 28–37; Stretto, *Kiasma*, Palazzo del Cinema.

MacNair, Andrew. "Chiasma." *Architecture & Urbanism* (October 1993): 64–71.

Norri, Marja-Ritta. "Holl's Helsinki Banana." *Architectural Review* (September 1993): 11; Museum of Contemporary Art, Helsinki.

Progressive Architecture (September 1993); Museum of Contemporary Art, Helsinki.

"The Art of Lighting or Lighting as an Art Form." *Light & Architecture* (September 1993): 30–35; D. E. Shaw.

Marpillero, Sandro. "Three Projects and the Antecedents." *Casabella* (September 1993): 4–19, 68–69, cover; selected projects.

"Construction in Four Parts." *Lotus* 77 (August 1993): 58–67; Texas Stretto House.

GA Houses 38 (July 1993): cover, 8–9, 32–59; Stretto House.

Louhenjoki, Pirkko-Liisa. "Close-Up on Steven Holl." *Arkkitehti* (April/May 1993): 17–31; selected projects, *Kiasma*.

"Meander Buildings." *Progressive Architecture* (March 1993): 26; Andrews University.

"GJ Forum." *GA Japan* 3 (Spring 1993): 274; Fukuoka.

Gorman, Jean. "Enlightened Reflection." *Interiors* (January 1993): 82–83; D. E. Shaw.

Taipale, Kaarin. "A Museum in Contexts." *Skala*

(1993): 58–61; *Kiasma*.

Broid, Isaac. "Bordes de la Cuidad." *Arquitectura* (January 1993): 52–65; Edge of a City.

1992

Morteo, Enrico. "Stretto House." *Domus* (December 1992): 56–65; Stretto House.

Zaera, Alejandro. "Towards an Aesthetic of Reappearance." *Quaderns* 197 (November/December 1992): 61–67.

"Edge of a City Projects."*Quaderns* 197 (November/December 1992): 78–87.

"Nexus World Kashii." *Japan Architect* (Winter 1992): 200–207.

Barna, Joel Warren and Michael Benedikt. "Stream & Consciousness." *Progressive Architecture* (November 1992): 54–63; Stretto House.

Barna, Joel Warren. "A House of Thought." *Texas Architect* (November 1992): 36–37; Stretto House.

"Societa Finanziaria D. E. Shaw." *Abitare* (October 1992): 207–12; D. E. Shaw.

Drewes, Frank F. "Der Stadtpoet: Steven Holl, N.Y." *Deutsche Bauzeitschrift* (September 1992): 1273–80; selected work.

"Steven Holl." *Fukuoka Style* (August 1992): 23; Fukuoka.

Sertl, William. "Seaside: Circa 1992." *Travel & Leisure* (August 1992): 79; Seaside Hybrid Building.

"Steven Holl: Fukuoka Hinged Space." *Architecture of Israel* (August 1992): cover, 12–14.

Muschamp, Herbert. "A Design That Taps Into the 'Informational City.'" *New York Times,* August 1992: 32; D. E. Shaw.

Stein, Karen D. "Virtual Reality." *Architectural Record* (June 1992): 114–19; D. E. Shaw.

Barriere, Philippe. "Lumieres Couleurs et Reflexions." *Architecture Interieure Cree* (April 1992): 156–57; D. E. Shaw.

"Architects We'd Hire: Our Top-Seven List." *Metropolitan Home* (April 1992): 149; Berkowitz-Odgis House.

"Un Quartier International a Fukuoka." *Architecture d'Aujourd'hui* (April 1992): 79–89.

Wortmann, Arthur. "Het Scheppend vermogen de schaalversnelling: de architectur van Steven Holl." *Archis* (April 1992): 27–35; Palazzo del Cinema.

Watanabe, Hiroshi. "Pasajes Japoneses: Una Investigcion de Steven Holl en Fukuoka." *Arquitectura Viva* (March–April 1992): 14–17.

Gallagher, John. "A New Era for Cranbrook." *Inland Architect* (March/April 1993): 25–26.

Green, Keith. "Steven Holl on the Edge of a City Exploration (Interview)." *Arcade* (March/April 1992): 7.

"Town Square, Four Houses, and Chapel, Port Ludlow, WA." *GA Houses* 34 (March 1992): 34–37.

Derossi, Pietro. "In the Circuit." *Lotus* 71 (February 1992): 36–41; Fukuoka.

Graaf, Vera. "Traumstadt am Meer." *Archtektur & Wohnen* (February 1992): 92–108; Seaside Hybrid Building.

Isozaki, Arata. "Project in Renga Form." *Lotus* 71 (February 1992): 42–50; Fukuoka.

"Bloque Holl." *DisenoInterior* (February 1992): 40–45; Fukuoka.

1991

Allen, Stan. "Architecture, Realism, Utopia: Steven Holl's Edge of A City." *Architecture & Urbanism* (December 1991): 4–7; Edge of A City: Phoenix and Cleveland.

"Stadtrander." *Archis Plus* (December 1991): 60–62; Edge of a City.

Cullen, Michael S. "Berlin: American Memorial Library Addition." *Competitions* (Winter 1991): 10–16.

Morteo, Enrico. *Domus* (October 1991): 42–51; Fukuoka.

Perlman, Ian. "The New City Message from Nexus World." *Kenchiku Bunka* (September 1991): 60–76; Fukuoka.

Di Battista, Nicola. "Biennale di Venezia." *Domus* (September 1991): 54–56.

Owen, Graham. "Projects: a film palace on the Lido." *Progressive Architecture* (September 1991): 142–145.

"Edge of A City: Two Projects by Steven Holl." *The New City* (Fall 1991): 133–36; Edge of A City, Cleveland and Phoenix.

"Fukuoka: Phenomenological...Steven Holl and Hideaki Ariizumi." *Japan Architect* (Autumn 1991): 92–103, 162–171; Fukuoka Housing.

Woodbridge, Sally B. "A Cross Cultural Concert in the Far East." *Progressive Architecture* (August 1991): 59–65; Fukuoka.

Nesbitt, Kate. "Cities of Desire/Boundaries of Cities." *Arquitectura* (August 1991): 116–121; Walker exhibition review.

Sullivan, C.C. "Directions of Urban Housing." *Space Design* (July 1991): 100, cover.

Gunts, Edward. "Holl Explores City's Edge at Walker." *Architecture* (June 1991): 33–34; Walker exhibition review.

Wright, Bruce. "Steven Holl in Walker's Last Look at Tomorrow." *Progressive Architecture* (June 1991): 28–29; Walker exhibition review.

"Architecture Tomorrow." *Design Quarterly* (1991): 3–48; Walker exhibition review.

Filler, Martin. "A Once Modest Architect Lets Out the Stops." *New York Times*, 26 May 1991: 28; Walker exhibition review.

"Quinta Monstra Internazionale di Architettura." *La Biennale di Venezia*, (September 1991): 102–117.

"Work in Progress." *Architectural Record* (April 1991): 134–37; Stretto House.

"Steven Holl Architects: Palazzo del Cinema." *GA Document* (April 1991): 48–49.

"1991 AIA Honor Awards." *Architecture* (March 1991): 65; Seaside Hybrid Building.

"Steven Holl: Stretto House." *GA Houses* 31 (February 1991): 6–11.

"38th PA Awards." *Progressive Architecture* (January 1991): 114–16; Fukuoka.

"Dallas Fort Worth, Texas, 1991, Spiroid Sectors." *Arquitectura* (January 1992): 81–84.

Mashburn, Joseph. "Living with the Land: a Case Study." *Modulus* (1991): 146–151.

1990

Technologia y Arquitecture (December 1990): 132–65; Berkowitz-Odgis House.

Nesbitt, Kate. "Steven Holl: An Interview." *Skala* (November 1990): 12–17.

Barriere, Philippe. *L'Architecture d'aujourd'hui* (October 1990): 122–26; three projects.

"House Echoes, Embraces Water," *Texas Architect* (September–October 1990): 44; Stretto House.

Tuomarla, Ulla. "Berlinin Kirjasto." *Arkkitehti* (May 1990): 92–99; four projects.

Pittel, Christine. "Master Alchemist," *Elle Decor* (May 1990): 92–99; four projects.

"L'Ampliamento delle American Memorial Library." *Industria delle Construzioni* (May 1990): 78–80.

"Steven Holl: Phenomenological Explorations in Architecture." *GSD News, Harvard University* (Spring 1990): 18.

"Steven Holl: Fukuoka." *GA Houses* 28 (March 1990): 50–53.

"Steven Holl a Berlino concorso per la American Memorial Library." *Domus* (February 1990): 1–3.

Branch, Mark Alden. "Switch in Berlin Library Competition." *Progressive Architecture* (February 1990): 21.

Stephens, Suzanne. "Berlin Library: Trading Places." *Oculus* (February 1990): 8–9.

"37th PA Awards." *Progressive Architecture* (January 1990): 80–85; Berlin AGB Library and College of Art and Landscape Architecture.

Hoffmann-Axthelm, Dieter and Klaus Bock. "American Memorial Library." *Bauwelt* (January 1990): 28–33.

Takiguchi, Norihiko. "Directions in Urban Housing, part II: Messages from Fukuoka." *Space Design* (January 1990): 53–84.

Balint, Juliana. "Ferienhaus am Atlantik." *Moebel Interior Design* (January 1990): 80–83; Berkowitz-Odgis House.

1989

Richardson, Martin. "Taking Pride of Place." *Building Design* (October 1989): 52–53; *Anchoring* book review.

Morteo, Enrico. "Steven Holl: Hybrid Building, Seaside, Fla." *Domus* (October 1989): 29–41; Fukuoka.

Woodbridge, Sally. "Mini-IBA." *Progressive Architecture* (October 1989): 39–40, 42.

"In Progress: Public and Campus Projects." *Progressive Architecture* (September 1989): 35–36; College of Architecture and Landscape Architecture, American Memorial Library.

"Anclar." *Quaderns d'Arquitectura i Urbanisme* (April–September 1989): 164–169; American Memorial Library.

"Anchoring: Project for Berlin." *Avant-garde* (Summer 1989): 92–99.

New York Architektur, 1970–1990, (August 1989): 148–52; five projects.

Dixon, John. "Seaside Ascetic." *Progressive Architecture* (August 1989): 59–67; Seaside.

Merkel, Jayne. "Contrasting Architectures: Holl- Ambasz at MoMA." *InLand Architect* (July/August 1989): 28,65.

Heck, Sandy. "Emilio Ambasz, Steven Holl: Architecture." *A + U* (July 1989): 3–14; review of MoMA exhibition.

"German-American Entente: Addition to the American Memorial Library in Berlin." *Architectural Record* (June 1989): 65.

Barriere, Philippe. "Ambasz et Holl au MoMA." *L'Architecture d'aujourd'hui*, (June 1989): 80; review of MoMA exhibition.

Shane, Grahame. "Steven Holl im MoMA." *Archithese* (May/June 1989): 73–77.

Iacucci, Paola. "Living within the heart of the Metropolis: Manhattan at the knife-edged point of Metropolitan Tower." *Abitare* 274 (May 1989): 194–201.

Architecture. (May 1989): 140–43; Berkowitz-Odgis House.

Phillips, Patricia C. "Steven Holl, Emilio Ambasz, MoMA." *Artforum* (May 1989): 148.

Ockman, Joann. "Interview with Steven Holl." *Columbia University Graduate School of Architecture, Planning, and Preservation Newsline* (April 1989).

Gastil, Raymond W. "Who's in and Who's out? Steven Holl and Emilio Ambasz." *Blueprint* (April 1989): 61, 63.

Kimball, Roger. "Holl and Ambasz, in a Manner of Speaking." *Architectural Record* (April 1989): 51–53; review of MoMA exhibition.

McDonough, Michael. "Emilio Ambasz and Steven Holl at MoMA." *ID Magazine* (March/April 1989): 70–71.

Fischer, Thomas. "Ambasz and Holl at MoMA." *Progressive Architecture* (March 1989): 33; review of MoMA exhibition.

Shane, Grahame. "Der Dekonstruktivismus und das Buch." *Archithese* (March 1989): 56–67.

"A Dreamer Who is Fussy About the Details." *Time Magazine* (20 March 1989): 75–77.

New York Times, 12 February 1989; review of MoMA exhibition.

"Synthesis." *The Architectural Review* (February 1989): 26–39; five projects.

"Vernacular." *The Architectural Review* (February 1989): 76–85.

Buchanan, Peter. "Holl Pressures." *The Architectural Review* (January 1989): 58–59; Giada.

Pasca, Vanni. "Le Costani del Progetto: Il Caso Steven Holl." *Casa Vogue* (January 1989): 66–85; Martha's Vineyard residence, Museum Tower Apt., Cohen Apt..,Giada, Pace Showroom.

Frampton, Kenneth. "Meet the Architect." *G.A. Houses* 25 (March 1989): 164–227; ten projects.

1988

Fischer, Thomas. "A Literary House." *Progressive Architecture* (December 1988): 62–67.

Filler, Martin and Elizabeth S. Byron, ed. "The Holl Truth." *House and Garden* (September 1988): 184–91, 245.

"House for Mr. and Mrs. B." *Utopica Two Architecture/Nature* (1988): 64–69.

"The Conviction of This Project Is..." *Off Ramp: SCI-Arc Journal.* Los Angeles: Southern California Institute of Architecture Press, 1988.

Russell, James S. "Skin and Bones." *Architectural Record* (mid-September 1988): 122–27; Metropolitan Tower Apartment.

"Baths: Steven Holl, New Forms for a Manhattan Make-over." *Architectural Digest* (April 1988): 42–43; Cohen Apartment.

"Architects Review Furniture: 7 Leading Architects Think About What Works, What Doesn't—And Why." *Architectural Digest* (August 1988): 52, 56.

"Awards." *Oculus* (March 1988): 6, 11.

"Three Projects." *A+U* (January 1988): 39–58.

1987

"Le Citta Imaginate." *XVII Triennale Di Milano Catalogue* . Milan: Electa, 1987, 292–95; Porta Vittoria.

"The Emerging Generation in the USA: Steven Holl." *GA Houses Special* 2 (November 1987): 92–97; Berkowitz-Odgis House.

Guerrera, Giuseppe. "Steven Holl." *New York Architects* (1987): 109–13.

"Porta Vittoria Project Area." *Lotus International* 54 (1987): 74–103.

Bethany, Marilyn. "What's Modern Now? Surprise Package." *New York* (28 September 1987): 64–67; Giada Clothing Shop.

Stein, Karen D. "Portfolio: Steven Holl Architects." *Architectural Record* (September 1987): cover, 90–101; Museum Tower Apartment, Giada Clothing Shop.

Bartle, Andrew and Jonathan Kirschenfeld. "The Analogous and the Anomalous Architecture and the Everyday: Young Eastern USA Architecture." *Ottagono* (September 1987): 20–47.

"Steven Holl: Houses." *El Croquis* (July 1987): 132–147.

Di Giorgio, Manola. "Una Piccola Galeria a Manhattan." *Domus* (June 1987): 5–6; Pace Collection Showroom.

"Showroom for the Pace Collection." *A+U* (May 1987): 89–94.

"Steven Holl, Three Projects." *AA Files* 14 (Spring 1987): 18–24; Porta Vitoria, Seaside Hybrid Building, Martha's Vineyard Residence.

Adams, Janet. "Re-Building New York: the Avant Garde Grows Up." *Blueprint* 35 (March 1987): 34–40.

"34th PA Awards." *Progressive Architecture* (January 1987): 108–09; Citation—Seaside Hybrid Building.

1986

Nicolin, Pierluigi, ed. "Bridge of Houses in Manhattan, Individual Characterizations, Urban Houses in North America." *Lotus International* 44 (1986): 41–50; projects and research.

McNair, Andrew. "40 Under 40." *Interiors* (September 1986): 175.

"Works: Steven Holl." *A+U* (August 1986): 59–74.

Nicolin, Pierluigi, ed. "Commercial Buildings with Residences Seaside." *Lotus International* 50 (1986): 27–29.

Smith, C. Ray. "Tale of Two Interiors." *Unique Homes / City Living* (June–July 1986).

"New York Showroom." *Nikkei Architecture* (May 1986): 82–87.

Gandee, Charles K. "Pace Maker" *Architectural Record* (April 1986): 93–103.

"Modern Redux: Critical Alternatives for Architecture in the Next Decade." *Grey Art Gallery, New York University* (March 1986); Berkowitz-Odgis House.

"Design Awards/Competitions: New York

Chapter/AIA Architecture Awards for Unbuilt Projects." *Architectural Record* (March 1986): 60–61.

"33rd PA Awards." *Progressive Architecture* (January 1986): 104–6; Citation Berkowitz-Odgis House.

"Expressions: 5 New Design Stores." *New York Times*, 16 January 1986, C-1.

Bethany, Marilyn. "Setting the Pace." *New York* (January 1986): 44–46.

1985

"Record Interiors, 1984." *Nikkei Architecture* (May 1985): cover, 179–84; Cohen Apartment.

Bartos, A. "A Humanistic Approach to Building Design." *Esquire* (December 1985): 84.

"Modernism Takes a New Turn." *Home Decorating* (Fall 1985): 30–35.

Davis, Douglas. *Newsweek* (12 August 1985): 64.

"Cohen Apartment." *Oculus* (May 1985): 3.

Greenstreet, Bob. "Law: Who Really Owns Your Designs." *Progressive Architecture* (April 1985): 63.

"Van Zandt house, East Hampton, NY." *Princeton Journal: Landscape* (1985): 125–127.

1984

Gandee, Charles K. "Homework:Cohen Apartment." *Architectural Record Interiors* (mid-September 1984): 156–63.

"Individual Characterizations: Houses for Craftsman on Staten Island 1980–84." *Lotus International* (1984): 44–45; Autonomous Artisans' Housing.

Phillips, Patricia C. "Steven Holl at Facade Gallery." *Artforum* (October 1984): 93; exhibition review.

Giovannini, Joseph. "An Unbuilt House Sets Up a Quandary." *New York TImes*, 18 October 1984; Van Zandt House.

"Teeter Totter Principles." *Perspecta—Yale Architectural Journal* 21 (1984): 30–51.

"Accent on Grandeur." *Newsweek* (3 September 1984): 70–71; Cohen Apartment.

Regnier, Constance. "Ein Kuehnes Experiment Mit 3 Deimensionen." *Ambiente* (August 1984): cover, 3, 118–27.

Bethany, Marilyn. "The Look of the 80s." *New*

York (16 April 1984): cover, 54–56.

"Architecture in Transition: Steven Holl." *Neue Architecktur: Sieben Junge Architekten aus Amerika, Deutchland, Endland und Italien.* (April 1984): 44–53; exhibition catalogue.

"31st PA Awards." *Progressive Architecture* (January 1984): 102–03; Van Zandt House.

1983

"Deposito de Casas de Seguridad/Estudio de Escultura y Casa de Baños." *Arquitectura* (September–October 1983): 66–68.

Viladas, Pilar. "Banca Rotunda." *Progressive Architecture* (September 1983): 100–03; Guardian Safe Depository.

Giovanni, Joseph. "Designers are Creating Etched Glass Renaissance." *New York Times*, 11 August 1983: C-1, C-10; sand-blasted glass.

Filler, Martin. "A Poetry of Place." *House & Garden* (May 1983): 78–81.

"Pont de Maisons: Projet pour Manhattan." *L'Architecture d'aujourd'hui* (February 1983): 9–10; Bridge of Houses.

1982

Iaccuci, Paola. "Projects: Poolhouse by Steven Holl." *Archetype* 2 (Fall 1982): 26–29.

Miller, Nory. "Braving the Elements." *Progressive Architecture* (July 1982): 78–81; Pool House & Sculpture Studio.

"Bridge of Houses, Melbourne Competition Design, 1979." *GA Houses 10* (1982): 131–133.

"Neue Tendenzen in den USA: Steven Holl." *Werk, Bauen & Wohnen* (May 1982): 40–43.

"Sculpture Studio, Scarsdale, NY, 1981." *A+U* (April 1982): 46–50.

"New Waves in American Architecture: 3." *GA Houses* 10 (March 1982): 128–37.

Weinstein, Edward. "Steven Holl: Hybrid Architect." *Arcade* (February–March 1982).

"29th PA Awards." *Progressive Architecture* (January 1982): 152–55; Citation—Metz House.

1981

Williams, Todd and Ricardo Scofidio. *Window, Room, Furniture: Projects.* New York: Rizzoli, 1981: 85.

Aida, Takefumi. "Steven Holl: New York." *A+U* (April 1981): 73–84.

Miller, Nory. "Interventions: Good Fences." *Progressive Architecture* (February 1981): 92–93; Millville.

1980

Emery, Marc. "Consultation Internationale sur le Quartier des Halles, Paris." *L'Architecture d'aujourd'hui* (April 1980): 7.

"Young Architects." *Yale School of Architecture, Gallery of Art and Architecture* (January 1980): 8; Telescope House.

1979

Maroni, Angioli. "Tre Edifici." *New Americans* (1979): 55.

Domus (December 1979): 7; Sokolov Retreat.

"Underwater House Project for Harbor of St. Tropez, France." *Archetype* 1 (Spring 1979): 29–30.

Battisti, Emilio. "Tre Giovano Architetti Americani." *Controspazio* (April 1979): 49–53.

"Retreat for M. Sokolov." *A+U* (February 1979): 22.

1978

Selig, M. "Gymnasium-Bridge: Checkerboard Site Plan to Signal Hope and Despair." *The Harlem River Yards: Bridging a South Bronx Community Need* (1978): 6–8.

"25th PA Awards: Haunting Image by a Young Architect." *Progressive Architecture* (January 1978): 81.

Architecture of Self-Help Communities. (January 1978): 66–71.

1977

"A New Wave of European Architecture." *A+U* (August 1977).

1976

Baumeister (October 1976): cover.

"Prelude au Congres de Vancouver Habitat '76." *L'Architecture d'aujourd'hui* (May–June 1976); 90–91.

Wagner, Walter F. "International Design Competition for the Urban Environment of

Developing Countries." *Architectural Record* 5 (May 1976): 136–39.

1973

Hilgenhurst, Ch. A. "Back from Niagara." *Architecture Plus* (April 1973): 74–75

AWARDS

1998 Alvar Aalto Medal

1998 National AIA Design Award
Chapel of St. Ignatius, Seattle University, Seattle, Washington

1997 Japanese Building Contractors Society Award

1997 National AIA Religious Architecture Award
Chapel of St. Ignatius, Seattle University, Seattle, Washington

1997 New York A.I.A. Medal of Honor

1996 Progressive Architecture Awards
Knut Hamsun Museum, Bodo, Norway
Museum of the City, Cassino, Italy

1995 NYC AIA Project Award
Cranbrook Institute of Science, Bloomfield Hills, Michigan
Honor Award, Chapel of St. Ignatius, Seattle University, Seattle, Washington

1993 NYC AIA Project Award
Makuhari Housing, Makuhari, Japan

1993 Graham Foundation Grant
Experimental Science Exhibition Design

1993 AIA National Honor Award
Stretto House, Dallas, Texas

1992 AIA National Honor Award
D. E. Shaw & Company Offices, New York, New York

1992 AIA New York Honor Award
Void Space / Hinged Space Housing, Fukuoka, Japan

1991 NYC Art Commission Excellence in Design Award
Renovation of the Strand Theater, Brooklyn, New York

1991 AIA National Honor Award
Hybrid Building, Seaside, Florida

1991 Progressive Architecture Award
Void Space/Hinged Space Housing, Fukuoka, Japan

1990 Arnold W. Brunner Prize in Architecture
American Academy and Institute of Arts and Letters

1990 Progressive Architecture Awards
College of Architecture and Landscape Architecture, University of Minnesota, Minneapolis, Minnesota
American Memorial Library, Berlin, Germany

1989 AIA National Honor Award
Berkowitz-Odgis House, Martha's Vineyard, Massachusetts

1988 NEA, Graham Foundation, and NYSCA Grants
MoMA Exhibition, New York, New York

1988 AIA New York Chapter Awards
Urban Proposal, Porta Vittoria District, Milan, Italy; Giada Clothing Shop, New York, New York

1987 Progressive Architecture Citation
Hybrid Building, Seaside, Florida

1986 Progressive Architecture Citation
Berkowitz-Odgis House, Martha's Vineyard, Massachusetts

1986 AIA New York Chapter Award
Pace Collection Showroom, New York, New York

1985 AIA New York Chapter Award
Andrew Cohen Apartment, New York, New York

1984 Progressive Architecture Citation
Van Zandt Weekend House, East Hampton, New York

1982 Progressive Architecture Citation
Metz House and Studio, Staten Island, New York

1978 Progressive Architecture Award
Gymnasium Bridge, Bronx, New York

EXHIBITIONS

Museum of Contemporary Art: *Present and Future: 100 Years of Architecture*, Los Angeles, California 1998.

GA Gallery: GA Exhibition, Tokyo, Japan, 1997.

Nederlands Architectuurinstituut: *Dutch Architecture and the American Model*, Rotterdam, The Netherlands 1997.

Venice Biennale: *Architect as Seismograph*, Venice, Italy 1996.

Centre de Cultura Contemporania de Barcelona: *Present and Futures: Architecture in Cities*, Barcelona, Spain, 1996.

Museum of Modern Art: *Light Construction*, New York, New York, 21 September 1995–2 January 1996 (group show).

Architectural League: *Kiasma,* New York, New York, 14 July–16 September 1995.

GA Gallery: *International '95*, Tokyo, Japan, 21 May–June 1995 (group show).

Spencer Museum of Art: *Unpainted to the Last*, Lawrence, Kansas, 19 August–8 October 1995 (group show); Martha's Vineyard Residence.

MAK, International Exhibition of Contemporary Architecture: *Manifestos*, Havana, Cuba, 29 December 1994–January 1995 (group show).

Museum für Gestaltung: *Jedes Haus ein Kunsthaus*, Zürich, Switzerland, 7 December 1994–5 February 1995.

Galerie ROM: *Steven Holl*, Oslo, Norway, 1–25 September 1994.

Galerie Für Architecture: *Steven Holl: Intertwining*, Hamburg, Germany, 1 July–15 August 1994.

Museum of Finnish Architecture: *Steven Holl*, Helsinki, Finland, 26 November–December 1993.

AR/GE Kunst—Galerie Museum: *Steven Holl*, Bolzano, Italy, September–October 1993.

Arc en Reve Centre d'Architecture: *Steven Holl*, Bordeaux, France, 18 June–31 August 1993.

Architektur Forum Zürich: *Context Japan: A Housing Experiment*, Zürich, Switzerland, 7 April–17 July (group show); Fukuoka Housing.

Arquitectos: *Steven Holl*, Madrid, Spain, 1 May–15 July 1993.

Center for the Fine Arts: *Miami, Architecture for the Tropics*, Miami, Florida, 19 December 1992–7 March 1993 (group show).

Arts Center de Singel: *Steven Holl,* Antwerp, Belgium, 7 October–15 November 1992.

Kansas City Art Institute: *Steven Holl*, Kansas City, MO, 1 June–30 August 1992.

Elysium Arts: *Steven Holl*, New York, NY, 8 July–3 August 1992.

K-2 Gallery: *Steven Holl*, Osaka, Japan, 23 July–9 August 1992.

GA Gallery: *Steven Holl*,Tokyo, Japan, 13 June–19 July 1992.

Sadock & Uzzan Galerie: *Steven Holl*, Paris,

France, 21 March–6 June 1992.

COAC: *Steven Holl*, Barcelona, Spain, 1 February–15 March 1993.

Canadian Center for Architecture: *Steven Holl*, Montreal, Canada, 24 February–March 1992.

Henry Art Gallery: *Projects in Architecture*, Seattle, Washington, 23 August–13 October 1991; Edge of a City.

Venice Biennale: *International Competition for New Palazzo del Cinema*, Venice, Italy, 8 September–6 October 1991 (group show).

Walker Art Center: *Edge of a City: Architecture Tomorrow*, Minneapolis, Minnesota, 21 April–23 June 1991.

Harvard Graduate School of Design: *Steven Holl: One or Two Buildings*, Cambridge, Massachusetts, 30 January–23 February 1990.

Aedes Gallery: *Steven Holl*, Berlin, Germany, 19 July–1 September, 1989.

Fukuoka Jisho Gallery: *Steven Holl*, Fukuoka, Japan, 30 May–1 September, 1989.

Werkebund Gallerie: *Steven Holl*, Frankfurt, Germany, 25 July–27 August, 1989.

Museum of Modern Art: *Steven Holl/ Emilio Ambasz*, New York, New York, February-April 1989.

GA Gallery: *Global Architecture-Houses*, Tokyo, Japan, 1987 (group show).

John Nichols Gallery: *House/Housing*, New York, New York, October–November 1987 (group show).

Grey Art Gallery: *Modern Redux: Critical Alternatives for Architecture in the Next Decade,* New York, NY, 4 March–19 April 1986 (group show).

VII Triennale of Milan: *Urban Section*, Milan, Italy, 1987 (group show).

Whitney Museum: *High Styles, American Design*, New York, New York, 1985 (group show).

Princeton School of Architecture: *Anchorage*, Princeton, New Jersey, Spring 1985.

Architecture in Transition: Berlin, Germany, October 1984.

Facade Gallery: *Cultural Connection and Modernity*, New York, New York, June 1984.

Whitney Museum Downtown: *Metamanhattan*, New York, New York, January 1984.

White Columns Gallery: *Bridge of Houses,* New York, New York, September 1982.

Architectura Arte Moderna: *Bridges,* Rome, Italy, December 1981.

Cooper Union: *Window, Room, Furniture*, New York, New York, December 1981 (group show).

Yale School of Architecture Gallery: *Young Architects*, New Haven, Connecticut, 14 January–1 February 1980 (group show).